MY BROTHER, HAIL AND FAREWELL!

By

Edward Zebrowski

To Ray —
all the best !

Ed Zebrowski

WOODSTOCK BOOKS

10-29-94

MY BROTHER, HAIL AND FAREWELL!

Library of Congress Catalog Card Number 94-60021

ISBN 0-9640096-0-9

Manufactured in the United States of America
First Printing 1994

Published by
WOODSTOCK BOOKS
Tampa, Florida

To My Brother, Stan, And All The Other Men Who
Fought On The Front Lines

Ode to a Dead Brother

By many lands and over many a wave
I come, my brother, to your piteous grave,
To bring you the last offering in death,
And o'er dumb dust expend an idle breath;
For fate has torn your living self from me,
And snatched you, brother, O, how cruelly!
Yet take these gifts, brought as our fathers bade
For sorrow's tribute to the passing shade;
A brother's tears have wet them o'er and o'er;
And so, my brother, hail, and farewell evermore!

Catullus 87-54 B.C.
tr. Sir Wm. Marris

Contents

Preface

Ever since I left the U.S. Army to enter Dartmouth College, I had planned to write a book about my experiences in the Intelligence and Reconnaissance Platoon of the 5th Infantry Regiment, 71st Division during World War II. I wanted this book to be about the individual soldier, his thoughts, frustrations, and his reactions to the many situations he confronted.

You will not find the analysis of grand strategies of war or the deployment of vast armies across the continent of Europe in this book. You will find ordinary soldiers like Bill Mauldin's Joe and Willie, complaining about everything with good reason and enduring every possible misery that men on the front lines could experience. Some of the events in this book have been rearranged for literary purposes and to conceal the identities of some of the men involved, but they all occurred in one form or another during the great upheaval we call World War II. I believe you will find the reading interesting.

EZ
Plainville, Connecticut
December, 1993

Acknowledgments

I am greatly indebted to my daughter, Jane, for the invaluable help, criticism, and support she had given me during the preparation of this book. I also received significant help from my two sons, Stephen and Edward; my wife, Elizabeth; and my sister, Sophie Lynch.

Dom Morelli, my old army buddy, answered all my telephone calls without complaint and helped to rekindle my memory regarding many of the incidents in this book.

Other army buddies who helped with the recollection of these events were Norm Rabek, Luther Joe Oleson, Ed Bowers, Jack Martin, Ruben Densman, Ralph Monsees, Elmont Michaelson, L.J. Richardson, and Francis Anterhaus. I am deeply indebted to all of these good friends.

December, 1993
Edward Zebrowski, M.D.
Plainville, Connecticut

Chapter 1

The Road to Glory?

McHugh was the first one to see the 88s after our platoon had stopped on a long wide curve just a few miles northeast of Steyr, Austria. We all got out of the jeeps to stretch our legs. McHugh had been in the lead jeep and I could see him standing on a slight rise in the road, scanning the edge of the woods with his field glasses, squinting against the sun.

I was in the last jeep wondering why we had stopped and then I saw the 88s, too. The Germans were busy loading the big guns and McHugh kept looking at them while all the other men started to scatter.

The first shell was a direct hit on our lead jeep. The blast lifted McHugh right out of his boots like a rag doll, tearing off both his legs. He was thrown thirty feet away and he lay there in the bright sunlight in the middle of the road, crying and bleeding to death. The Germans then covered the area with a scathing concentration of machine gun fire. There was no way we could get to him.

When that first shell landed, most of us followed Sgt. Brawley into the thick-walled pigsty that was attached to one of the farmhouses along the road. We could hear the frightening cracking of the bullets as they passed over our heads and the clattering as they slammed into the concrete walls of the house. The jeeps, with their motors still running, were parked where we'd left them in the middle of the road, with our rifles concealed under canvas on the floor.

We lay on the concrete floor on dried-up manure, listening to McHugh moaning and crying for help. The shelling continued and the machine guns kept up with their high-pitched rapid staccato bursts, sending shivers up our spines.

"This is one helluva mess we've gotten into this time," Sgt. Brawley said, looking out one of the small dirty windows. "And I don't want any of you birds trying to go out there to get McHugh. You'll never make it with that machine gun firing."

He grunted, his lower lip sticking out a mile.

****

We had been on duty for about two months, our mission being to reconnoiter the territory in front of the line battalions. We were supposed to contact the Germans surreptitiously, but not to engage them in combat if we could avoid it. The information we gathered was then relayed to S2, regimental intelligence, who directed the line battalions in their clean-up operations.

We were members of the Intelligence and Reconnaissance Platoon of the Fifth Infantry Regiment, Seventy-first Division, a small platoon of twenty men in Patton's Third Army. We were part of a huge assault force of four hundred and forty thousand men plunging through the heart of Germany in headlong pursuit of the rapidly retreating Germans. By May 1, 1945, with a light snow falling intermittently, we seized the dam at Braunau on the Inn River with only one tanker killed in action by a lone sniper. Braunau, a small town situated on the Austrian border, was Adolf Hitler's birthplace. From that moment on, it seemed the end of the war was very near.

Over the next three days, we covered approximately eighty kilometers, driving a wedge deep into the Austrian countryside through Altheim, Reid, and Pramerdorf. On May 4, without one shot being fired, we took Lambach, liberating the poor bastards who had been living in the hell of Gunskirchen Lager. Hitler had attended elementary school in this village. The townspeople, mostly women and children with only a scattering of old men, greeted us with the usual white bed sheets and pillow cases fluttering out of their windows as a sign of surrender. By then we had penetrated farther east than any other unit in all the allied armies in the European Theater of War.

On Saturday, May 5, 1945, with the day breaking bright and clear, we were surprised with new and unusual orders.

"Get your weapons under cover," Sgt. Brawley said. "Remove the .50 caliber machine gun."

Morelli, one of our drivers, was already in his jeep.

"What the hell's going on, Sergeant?" he asked.

"This is a special mission and we have to appear totally unarmed," Brawley answered.

Colonel Simon C. Wofford, the commanding officer of the Fifth Infantry Regiment stood by his jeep, shading his eyes against the sun, impatiently tapping his riding crop against his right thigh. The holster with his .45 was conspicuously absent. His driver, Ed Bowers, waved to us.

Wofford's plan was to penetrate fifty kilometers into enemy territory, acting throughout the mission as if the war had ended. Our destination was Steyr, Austria, where we were supposed to meet the Russians at the Enns River. He was counting heavily on the element of surprise to help us complete our mission.

Besides Colonel Wofford, there were Major Irwin S. Booker from S2, two newspaper correspondents, and one photographer in our group. This added baggage, apparently, was brought along to verify the audacity of the mission when it came time to distribute medals for valor. It seemed Patton and Montgomery were not the only ones who could play soldier and strut across the military horizon. Time was running out. The war was coming to an end and Wofford felt he had to act quickly

To add to the deception that the war had really ended, the colonel included a prisoner of war in his jeep, a captured SS colonel of the 12th SS Standarte (regiment).

With the announcement of Hitler's death in Berlin on April 30, 1945, the German and Austrian people were in a state of mourning. They were crying openly and unashamedly. With this emotional reaction sweeping what was left of the Third Reich, Colonel Wofford felt the German soldiers were ready to call it quits. Furthermore, most of the German people thought that once the German Army capitulated, Patton would make it a part of his Third Army and proceed immediately into combat against the Russians. Every day we saw increasing numbers of Germans rapidly moving west to escape capture by the Russians, who were already fighting in the streets of Vienna.

Colonel Wofford took one more precaution to ensure the success of this daring mission. He had ordered a motorized battalion of infantry to follow us approximately four hours behind, with another battalion on foot.

Now if only the Germans cooperated, we hoped to complete our mission without a single casualty. Unfortunately, we were not that lucky.

I shoved my M1 under the canvas on the floor of the jeep, feeling very uneasy. I saw the look of concern on the faces of the other men. I knew they felt the same way. Morelli was in one of the jeeps ahead of me. He kept getting out of his vehicle and rearranging the rifles on the floor in the rear of his jeep. He looked back and gave me the thumbs-up sign.

Uncertainty was part of every one of our missions. Would there be inadvertent contact with the enemy? And if so, how many Germans would be involved? Would they be willing to surrender or would we encounter units trained to fight to the last man? Would they be well equipped and supported with armored units, 88s, machine guns, panzerfausts (bazookas), or any of the other excellent weapons capable of finishing us off? Were there pockets of Waffen SS ahead of us or just regular army units, the Wehrmacht? We knew the SS were much more inclined to put up a significant battle, being elite troops totally dedicated to Hitler.

We had learned to live with a certain amount of raw fear. It was good to be afraid in battle. The fear sharpened our senses and quickened our responses, enabling us to get through a particularly grueling encounter.

We knew, too, that once an action began, the fear would be muted, perhaps disappearing altogether, and we would respond like the well-trained soldiers we were, or thought we were. Our fellow platoon members expected us to act in a certain way under certain circumstances. This feeling was stronger than any fear we could experience. We were aware that fear was a normal reaction and that the adrenaline coursing through our bodies would keep us alive long enough to accomplish what we had to do, even though our hearts felt as if they would burst through our chests.

Our usual patrol consisted of five jeeps and twenty men. On this day we had a caravan of ten jeeps and about forty men. I patted the Luger I had concealed in a shoulder holster and felt somewhat better, even though we had been warned that if the enemy soldiers captured us with German pistols in our possession, they would immediately execute us. I decided to take my chances. I noticed the other men were checking their pistols, too.

At first, everything went along smoothly. It was a bright sunny day. The people in the villages along our route had not really experienced the savagery or brutality of the war, even though they had, within a few kilometers of their surroundings, one of the most atrocious concentration camps on this earth, Gunskirchen Lager. They were out doing their usual Saturday chores. Steyr seemed far away.

We stopped briefly in each village and spoke to the people in what little German we knew.

"Krieg kaputt," we said repeatedly. The war is over.

"Grüse Gott," they would reply, God's greeting, making the sign of the cross and hurrying away, fear, astonishment, and bewilderment plainly showing on their faces. Everywhere we looked, there were white sheets hanging from the windows, billowing out in a gentle breeze.

We didn't forget, however, the slaughter that took place as the 71st Division approached Regensburg, when the entire I and R Platoon of the Fourteenth Infantry Regiment was wiped out in a matter of minutes while white sheets were flying all over the place.

But we kept it up.

"Krieg kaputt."

"Grüse Gott."

It almost appeared to be rehearsed, a learned response. That's the way it went for the first few hours. We didn't see any soldiers around and everybody was extremely pleasant and polite.

Suddenly, as we swung through one of the larger towns, Wels, we found ourselves in the middle of a German military convoy, both columns having converged on a square in the middle of town. Truck after truck moved slowly through the streets, loaded with German soldiers peering out with completely blank expressions on their faces. There were many horse-drawn wagons, the animals gaunt and poorly kept, followed by hundreds of bedraggled infantrymen, looking tired, exhausted, walking like an army of robots, their clothes dirty and in total disarray, remnants of a ragged and worn-out army. There were only a few pieces of light artillery dragging behind some of the trucks. Most of the units appeared to be Hungarian.

We were just as shocked as the policeman in the center of the town square, who was standing on a wooden platform directing traffic, his eyes bulging with surprise.

"Krieg kaputt," we yelled out as we passed him, waving our hands and smiling.

The whistle fell out of his mouth, his arms frozen in the direction of the traffic, a look of utter disbelief on his face.

We continued with the convoy for about one kilometer and then turned east toward Steyr. By then we had become much bolder, almost convincing ourselves that the war, indeed, had ended.

In the next village, Kremsmunster, there were a few German soldiers walking along both sides of the road. Many of them were officers with holstered pistols hanging from their belts. When we stopped briefly at one point, I saw one of our men jump from the jeep ahead of us, run up to a German officer and say, "Krieg kaputt." He then put out his hand and said, "Pistole." The German hesitated a moment, shifting his gaze to us in the jeeps. He then took out his pistol and handed it over. It was like watching a rehearsal of a movie.

Soon, we were all doing the same thing. In a relatively short time, we had over a dozen pistols in every jeep. Most of them were Lugers and P38s, but we also garnered some Berettas, Walther 7.35s, Mausers, and some old Hungarian semiautomatics that looked like they had been manufactured during World War I.

Instead of a dangerous mission deep in enemy territory, this seemed to be a part of a Saturday picnic excursion in the beautiful Austrian countryside. But it didn't stay that way for long.

In the next village, Bad Hall, we again stopped for a short time. One of the newspaper correspondents ran up to a tall blond SS trooper and said the familiar words, "Krieg kaputt, pistole," extending his hand to receive the gun. The SS trooper, without one moment's hesitation, pulled out his Luger, aimed pointblank at the man's chest and fired three times. The man crumpled to the ground, clutching his chest, a startled look on his face. The trooper then deliberately and slowly shifted his gaze to us in the jeeps with a look of utter contempt on his face. He returned the Luger to its holster in a sweeping grandiose motion and then turned and walked away, as if daring us to do anything about it.

"Don't move," Sgt. Brawley said in a hoarse whisper as we instinctively went for our rifles under the canvas cover. "There are too many of them here."

Suddenly, from out of nowhere, the street was full of German soldiers. They were no longer walking by. They stood there looking at us silently, waiting to see what we were going to do. Some of them started to move in closer. "Doc" Neuman, our medic, had already run over to the mortally wounded man and was busy applying bandages to his chest to stop the bleeding. Brawley told Doc to stay with him and wait for the motorized battalion that was coming up behind us.

"That's a great idea," Doc said sarcastically, looking at his watch. "That will help this guy a lot."

"Nothing's going to help him," Brawley said.

We pulled away slowly and quietly, leaving Doc looking over his shoulder at us, a lone and forlorn figure huddled over the injured man lying in the street. The rest of the jeeps were already far ahead of us.

Only then did Sgt. Brawley turn around and growl, "Jesus Christ! I never saw a more stupid bunch of bastards in my whole life. 'Krieg kaputt, pistole.' It's lucky we all didn't get our asses shot off in that town."

"If you thought it was so stupid," I blurted out, "why didn't you stop us before that poor son-of-a-bitch was shot by that SS trooper?"

"Shut up, Zebrowski," Brawley yelled back.

He turned away from us, totally disgusted, still muttering under his breath. He looked up the dust-filled road to make sure we were not too far behind the jeep ahead of us. He knew the Germans liked to knock off the last jeep of a patrol and that was a constant worry to him.

A few minutes later, he leaned over to touch the two Lugers and the P-38 he had stowed under the front seat that we had given him. We could see this made him feel better.

It took us about six hours to reach the outskirts of Steyr. We stopped there for about thirty minutes and six RAF pilots came over to our jeep to greet us. I was just about to say the magic words "Krieg kaputt," when one of them yelled out, "How's the war going, chaps?" They had been taken prisoner five years before, having been shot down in a raid over Dunkirk. They had been working in the fields as farm laborers and had been fairly well-treated, even though their rations of bread and soup were skimpy. We were happy to give them all our K rations. Up to that time we had been living off the land, eating chicken, eggs, and venison, supplemented by all the dark bread we could find. We told them to wait for the motorized battalion behind us. We then took off into the center of Steyr. There were two main bridges crossing the Enns River in that area. The Russians were nowhere in sight.

Our basic mission had been completed, penetrating into enemy territory nearly fifty kilometers with only one casualty. The ruse of concealing our weapons and not engaging any of the soldiers we had met had worked without a hitch.

But then Colonel Wofford made his first mistake. Not being happy just sitting and waiting for the rest of the troops to catch up with us, he decided to move on.

After waiting thirty minutes or so, discussing the situation with Major Booker, he directed the lead jeep to move out north of the city. Again white sheets were decorating all the houses. As we drove up a long hill leading out of town, we saw dozens of Hitler Jungen, about twelve to fourteen years of age, in full uniform. They carried submachine guns slung from their shoulders, looking very determined, as if the fate of the nation rested on them alone. They didn't pay any attention to us and we wasted no time getting past them. We didn't relish getting into a shooting match with a bunch of kids, especially since our weapons were concealed and they were ready to fire with submachine guns. Colonel Wofford wouldn't have been happy surrendering to a gang of children. He would never have lived it down, preferring death to such an ignominious event. There are no medals for that kind of action.

We had driven only four kilometers north of Steyr, heading toward Dietachdorf on the east side of the Enns River, when what we thought was a stray shell exploded on the cab of an old German truck. The farmer had pulled up on the side of the road in front of an old barn full of hay. There was no swoosh, just one big blast. We had always been taught that as long as we heard a long swoosh, we had nothing to worry about. A short swoosh and a blast was dangerously close. If you didn't hear a swoosh, that meant the shell had your name on it. Of course, in that case you didn't have anything to worry about, either, because by then you'd have been blasted into tiny bits flying through the air. As we passed the truck, we saw the driver still sitting erect behind the steering wheel, but his head was gone.

Like a bunch of fools we kept on, following the jeep in front of us. Without fear, a combat infantryman is totally defenseless. He might as well be naked in front of a firing squad.

We drove along for another hundred yards or so and then stopped about fifty feet in back of Morelli's jeep. The gravity of the situation still didn't penetrate our brains, which were numbed by the hot sun and so many exclamations of "Krieg kaputt" and "Grüse Gott." We had been lulled into a false sense of security, a deadly condition for a soldier. I got out of the jeep in no particular hurry and saw McHugh about two hundred yards ahead of us. He was standing there with his field glasses trained at the woods to our right. I grabbed my glasses to take a look.

"Holy shit," I yelled out. "Those bastards are shooting 88s at us."

Just then a shell struck the lead jeep, hurling McHugh into the air, tearing his legs off and leaving him bleeding to death in the bright sunlight. This was quickly followed by another shell that ripped open a big hole in the roof of one of the cement farmhouses along the road, blasting half the orange tile high into the air. The debris came crashing down on the jeeps.

The Germans swept the area methodically with machine gun fire. We made our mad dash for the safety of the thick-walled pigsty with no time to take our weapons from underneath the canvas in the jeeps or even shut off the engines.

Fortunately, there were no pigs in the pig pen. A few chickens were clucking around, upset because we had invaded their home. The machine guns let up their high-pitched chatter periodically. During those moments of relative silence, we could hear McHugh crying and calling for help. We heard a jeep roar into action during one of those lulls and we rushed to the windows just in time to see Colonel Wofford and his driver take off back to Steyr. Major Booker came in from the rear of the building.

"Colonel Wofford has just gone back to Steyr," he said, "to contact the motorized battalion that's on the way. He'll coordinate everything better from that vantage point than from here. In the meantime, I'll be in charge in his absence."

"Couldn't he reach them by radio, sir?" I asked.

He ignored my question with a contemptuous glance and went over to Sgt. Brawley and whispered something to him.

A German soldier suddenly appeared in the doorway carrying a white flag. Nobody had noticed him coming until he was standing in front of us. He couldn't have been over sixteen.

"My commanding officer demands your immediate surrender," he said in faultless English. He had a note in his right hand.

"Bullshit," Major Booker said.

He pulled his .45 from a shoulder holster and shot the young soldier between the eyes.

"Drag his body outside," he said. "As far as you're all concerned, he was armed."

I slipped out the back and crawled over the road to the trench Morelli had jumped into. He had squeezed himself into the pit with his head deep in the corner. He turned quickly to look at me, spitting dirt out of his mouth.

"What was that shot I heard coming from the house?"

"Booker just shot a young German soldier carrying a white flag. They're demanding our surrender. Booker will probably get a Distinguished Service Medal for that valiant act, especially if he writes the citation himself."

"Let's try to get McHugh," Morelli said, still spitting out specks of dirt. "He's bleeding to death and I can't stand him crying like that."

We crawled down the road, watching the machine gun bullets kicking up the dirt just a few feet away from us. As we crawled past another slit trench, Sgt. MacKay popped his head out.

"Am I glad to see you guys!" he said. "I'm in here with a German soldier. He says if the Germans get here first, I'm his prisoner, and if the Americans come first, he's my prisoner."

"You're safe in that trench," I said. "Stay there. Booker said Wofford went for the motorized battalion. We'll know who is going to be whose prisoner in about two to three more hours."

We finally got to McHugh just as he was taking his last few breaths. It was miserable. There was nothing left of his legs.

"You know, Morelli," I said, my voice breaking, "McHugh told me he was going to study to be a minister when he got out of the service. And then he was going to marry his high-school sweetheart, Ellen, a girl he'd known ever since he was a kid. He just got out of the hospital yesterday after having had an attack of pneumonia. He told me he was so happy to be back with the platoon."

"Yeah," Morelli said. "Stop talking, will you, Zeb?"

I looked at him. He had tears in his eyes. I turned away quickly, feeling rotten.

The machine gunner let up for a while, but just like clockwork an 88 shell was sent over about every ten minutes. The buildings were gradually crumbling.

"Let's get the hell out of here while the German machine gunner is taking a piss break," Morelli said.

We crawled back to the pigpen.

"Where the hell did you guys go?" Brawley yelled out as soon as we got back. "I told you to stay here."

"We had to take a piss," I said.

"Don't be a smart ass," Brawley said. "I saw both of you crawl down the road to where McHugh was lying. That was taking an unnecessary risk. There was nothing you could do for him. Is he dead?"

"Yeah, he's dead. And he died by himself."

"Everybody has to die by himself. It's not easier to do it with everybody staring at you. That was a stupid thing to do, you know. You're lucky that machine gunner didn't pick you guys off."

Brawley handed me a flare gun.

"What's this for?" I asked.

"I want you and Morelli to take off to that abandoned farmhouse at the intersection about a mile down the road."

"What for?" Morelli said. "Do you want that machine gunner to have another chance at us, Sergeant?"

"All I need is another smart ass," Brawley said. "I want you to shoot this flare off if the Germans get there before Colonel Wofford gets back with our motorized battalion. If Wofford gets back first, you can tell him our location in the pigpen so he doesn't blow us all to hell with mortar fire."

"If the pigpen is still standing," I said.

"In about thirty minutes, there won't be anything left to your little hideaway," Morelli said. "And our motorized battalion won't be here for another two to three hours, Sergeant. And when the Germans see that dead kid with the white flag that Booker knocked off, that will be good-by to Mrs. Brawley's blue-eyed boy."

Brawley didn't look too happy.

"Move out," he barked.

Morelli and I crouched down and made our way back to the jeeps to retrieve our M1s.

"This is stupid, you know, Morelli," I said. "We have to go a mile under open fire from a German machine gunner while that son-of-a-bitch is back there shivering behind walls that are two feet of solid concrete."

"The 88s will soon level every one of those buildings," Morelli said, "and then his ass will be out in the open just like ours."

Although the firing continued intermittently, we did some good broken-field running, flopping to the ground every ten to fifteen yards. We then crawled so that we wouldn't get up at the same spot we hit the ground. We reached the house in about thirty minutes, amazingly unscathed except for the bruises we incurred hitting the ground. Both of us had expected to be killed.

Looking back, we saw the upper sections of the houses already demolished. Because of a slight rise in front of the houses, the Germans couldn't get a good bead on the lower parts of the pigpen where the rest of the platoon was hiding.

"It looks like our two heroes, Brawley and Booker, are going to make it after all," I said.

We were pinned down for a total of four hours before we saw the advance units of the motorized battalion drive into view. We breathed much more easily after that. Mortars were immediately set up and Morelli and I just sat there and watched in amazement how incredibly efficient our 71st Division was. Between the tanks with their new 76mm guns and the mortars, it was all over in one hour. The Germans came out of their emplacements with their hands on top of their heads.

It was early evening by the time we started walking back to Steyr. Our joy at coming out of this mission alive was tempered by the sadness of McHugh's death. We kept hearing that awful crying in the middle of the road as the shelling ripped apart the buildings we were in and the machine guns sprayed the area. There was nothing we could do. He died alone in the middle of the road.

Halfway back to Steyr, we saw our company clerk, Corporal Majchack plodding up the hill. When he saw me alive and well, he nearly collapsed. Shortly before coming up the hill to meet our platoon, he had received a preliminary report that I had been killed by a direct hit with an 88. When he told me that, I paraphrased Mark Twain and said that report was grossly exaggerated.

After a lot of backslapping, all of us being overwhelmed by the sheer joy of escaping death, Morelli gave Majchack one of the pistols we had picked up on this mission. Majchack closed his eyes tightly and, pointing the weapon at the ground, pulled the trigger. The bullet went right through his right big toe. He protested loudly that it wasn't intentional as he danced around on one foot, howling like a wounded dog.

Three days later, on May 8, 1945, the war was officially over. The Russians didn't arrive at the Enns River until May 9. There was absolutely no reason for Colonel Wofford to make that mad dash fifty kilometers through enemy territory. We later learned that our lead jeep actually went past the first 88 stationed near the road. That 88 was knocked out by the same shell that killed McHugh. That's why

MacKay and a German soldier ended up sharing the same fox hole.

We lost a good man from our platoon as well as an American correspondent. A young German soldier lost his life carrying a white flag. Colonel Wofford and Major Booker just wanted to play soldier before the war really ended.

Our division, the 71st, that had been trained with mules in Colorado, traveled over eight hundred miles in approximately two months. We were officially recognized as having penetrated farther east than any other unit in the allied forces in Europe. We captured over 107,000 German soldiers. Three hundred of our own men were killed in battle.

Although our Intelligence and Reconnaissance Platoon ended our last mission just northeast of Steyr, the 71st Division Recon Troop had orders on May 6 and 7 to continue eastward in one more final attempt to meet the Russians. They were the only men of Patton's Third Army still actively engaging the enemy when the war officially ended.

The roads were so jammed with German soldiers retreating from the advancing Russians that the 71st Recon Troop only reached Amstett and Waidhofen, still thirty-eight miles from the most westward point of the Russian Army.

During that time, our platoon settled down in Steyr for some well-deserved rest.

Chapter 2

Bitching in Bitche

"**W**hat's this?" Morelli asked, pointing to the single clip of ammunition.

"That's your ammo, soldier. What the hell do you think it is? Keep moving."

Sgt. Brook, the supply sergeant, was in no mood for any discussion. I was right behind Morelli and I could see the tension on Brook's face.

"One clip, eight rounds?" Morelli kept on. He wasn't going to give up just because Sgt. Brook was jittery and irritable.

"You're kidding, aren't you? You mean we're supposed to take on the entire German Army with one clip of ammunition?"

"That's all I'm authorized to give you. Keep moving. You're slowing down the line."

Brook was scowling now, his voice a little louder and rougher.

"You'll probably get the rest by the end of the week," he added, "if the Germans don't get you by then."

"What a comforting thought," I said. "You certainly inspire confidence in our military supply system, Sergeant."

"I no got, you no get. I got, you get."

Sgt. Brook did a good job imitating our first sergeant, Sgt. Colombresi, who spoke nothing but fractured English.

"I suppose we can wait until we see the whites of their eyes," I said, taking my single clip of eight rounds of .30 caliber M1 ammunition from the sergeant.

"Yeah," Morelli said. "Then you'd better have your bayonet

ready the way you shoot, Zeb, or you can kiss your ass good-by."

We were in Bitche, France, just east of Nancy, in the process of relieving the 100th Infantry Division that had been dug in on a stationary front facing the Germans. This was our first day on the front and everybody was nervous and jittery. We were joking and kidding around, but being issued one clip of ammunition only added to the tension we already felt.

Sgt. Brawley was waiting for us at the end of the line, growling at everybody as usual.

"Stop bitching about the ammo," he said. "It won't do you any good. If we had the ammunition, you'd get it, like Sgt. Brook said. But we don't have it, so that's that."

Morelli and I continued to horse around and tease each other, but everything seemed to fall flat, especially with many of the older guys looking like this was the last day on the earth.

"Corporal Stulek is with the men from the 100th right now," Brawley said, "getting oriented and getting the exact location of our OP. In fact, he should be at the OP this very minute."

He looked at his watch.

"He's scheduled to be back in an hour and he'll lead us to where we're supposed to go. In the meantime, the kitchen is open, so get some coffee and chow. It'll be K rations for some time after this."

He turned toward the mess tent.

"And don't wander around," he added over his shoulder. "I want all of you ready to move out at a moment's notice."

It was March 11, 1945, just about six weeks after we had landed in LeHavre, Normandy. We were still weak-kneed from the bad food the navy had given us while crossing the Atlantic on the USS General Bliss.

We had shipped out from Fort Benning, Georgia, by train on January 4, 1945. We had gotten to the station on trucks at 6:00 a.m. and were scheduled to depart at 8:00. Unfortunately, the train didn't pull out until 8:00 a.m. the next day. All of us were in a rotten mood, lying on the floor with all our equipment, nibbling K rations, grumbling, and pissing up against the side of the train station. There were thousands of us huddled together, absolutely convinced we were being led by a totally inept group of officers and heading towards doomsday.

The train finally pulled out for the cold, frozen north, emitting dreary shrieks as it rattled out of the station, our destination Camp Kilmer, New Jersey.

We relaxed at Camp Kilmer for a few days, ate some good food, and listened to Bing Crosby and the Andrews Sisters singing, "Don't Fence Me In." We finally boarded the USS General Bliss at 6:00 a.m. on a freezing morning, January 11, 1945, with the temperature hovering around zero. There was a bitter cold that penetrated our bones. An army band was huddled to one side, apparently to send us off with some stirring Sousa marches. It was too cold to play their instruments, so they stood cursing the fools who sent them there. Instead of playing, they accompanied us with a dreary, god-forsaken beat from the base drum. It was a rhythm fit for a grand funeral procession.

The I and R Platoon of Headquarters Company was holed up in Seven Charlie, the bottom compartment of the ship, crammed in elbow to elbow, ass to ass. Half the men became seasick as soon as we pulled out of the harbor. There was a smell of vomit and sweat hanging heavy in the air.

Seven Charlie was the last compartment to be called for chow. By the time we got to the mess hall, there was nothing left to eat but greasy, smelly slop. A quarter of the men landed in the ship's infirmary with severe stomach cramps, vomiting, and diarrhea. Morelli and I were part of that unlucky group.

Morelli rolled over side to side, holding his belly while vomiting into a basin.

"I'm dying, Zeb," he groaned. "I'll never get to fight the Germans. I've been done in by the U.S. Navy."

"Burial at sea is one of the nicer navy ceremonies," I said, trying to keep his spirits up while holding onto my own grumbling belly.

"If they sent this food over to the German Army," Morelli said, "the war would have been over long ago."

"I think they're planning to do just that, but they wanted to try it out on us first to see if it really works."

All of us survived that naval assault on our gastrointestinal tracts, but the abdominal cramps, nausea, and diarrhea lingered on in sporadic bouts, constantly reminding us what a powerfully destructive force navy cooks could be.

We anchored in Southampton harbor in England overnight and crossed the Channel the next day, landing at LeHavre about ten o'clock at night.

The harbor had been leveled flat by devastating bombardment previously, but that night the whole area was flooded with bright lights. Either there was no fear of the German Luftwaffe or plain military stupidity was again in glorious exhibition. We were loaded down with what felt like a thousand pounds of gear: full field pack, blanket roll, heavy winter overcoat, rifle, helmet, and gas mask. With rubbery legs we made our way carefully down the gangplank. We disembarked on floating docks and climbed directly into waiting two-and-one-half-ton trucks, packed in like fish in a barrel of ice.

We roared off into the Normandy countryside, cold, tired, and hungry. We rolled along for an hour or so, through narrow, winding streets of darkened villages, the trucks nearly brushing up against the concrete walls and metal balconies of the shadowy buildings. Up hills, down hills, gears grinding, the lumbering vehicles slowed down to a near halt, engines whining, and then speeded up again with a growl and finally stopped. We could hear some men talking in the distance, but couldn't make out the words. Truck doors slammed shut and we were off again into the blackness of the night, the trucks lurching around corners, the men groaning and complaining as we leaned against one another and tried to maintain our balance, our legs cold and numb.

We finally reached our destination just as it started to get light, bone-weary after eight hours of rolling through the French countryside. It was only later that we found out we were in St. Laurent en Caux, about ten miles from where we began our journey. We had been lost all night, going around in circles.

We stared at one another, bleary-eyed, stiff-legged and miserable, as we got out of the trucks, our backs breaking with pain. We marched off to our designated tents in the early morning light.

The newspapers would have described us as fresh troops, young, eager, vibrant, full of excitement and anticipation, and ready to engage the enemy on a moment's notice. Horseshit! We were shivering with cold, exhausted, sleepy, hungry and nauseated at the same time, belching, bloated with gas and suffering terrible pangs of heartburn. Our bladders were riding high around our ears and we were thoroughly disgusted with our so-called leaders. These were the men who were going to lead us into battle. That was enough to scare anybody shitless. We collapsed onto our folding cots in our pyramidal tents, fully clothed, forgetting about the war and our individual miseries and misgivings and promptly went to sleep.

We found out very quickly that the cold, damp weather of Normandy made it difficult to control our bladders. The latrine was situated about one hundred yards beyond the company area. That was too damned far to walk in the middle of the night for a quick piss. So all of us got #10 cans from the kitchen that we kept under our cots. We emptied them every morning outside the tent until the whole place smelled like one big urinal.

Sam Brawley was especially irritable for some reason at this time. He was constantly bitching at us for one thing or another. Nobody could please him. One night after using his piss can in the middle of the night, he went into the worst rage we had ever seen. He woke up all the men in the tent, growling and cursing, his lower lip out a mile.

"If I ever catch the son-of-a-bitch who put holes in the bottom of my piss can," he said, "he's a dead man."

He had been leaning over his cot when he was using his can and all his blankets got soaked.

After a day of grumbling and threatening, however, he let up on us and was a little easier to live with. Morelli looked at me and I looked at him. We never did find out who it was, but all the men felt whoever it was should have received some kind of special citation for an exceptionally valorous deed. We recognized, of course, how difficult it would have been to write such a commendation without the entire company falling to the ground in a convulsion of laughter.

Soon after that, Capt. Davis of Headquarters Company made an inspection tour of the company area and outlawed the use of piss cans.

Morelli and I continued to have bouts of misery with our intestinal tracts, suffering with cramps and diarrhea off and on for the next several weeks. It was a long haul to the latrine. One night when I was especially sleepy, I started from the edge of the company area intending to go directly through the darkness to the company outhouse. No lights were permitted and there was no moon. It was utterly black. I knew I had to travel about one hundred yards, but it seemed much longer. I didn't realize that I had veered off to my right and was actually doing my duty in the adjacent company's latrine. When I started back, I again drifted off to my left and soon found myself sloshing through a marsh covered with about one to two feet of water. I was cold, miserable, and swearing a blue streak. The swearing served two purposes. It helped to relieve my frustration and at the same time alerted the guard so he wouldn't shoot me. I finally reached the road, thoroughly soaked.

A voice boomed out of the blackness: "Don't move or you're dead."

Being new in a war zone, everybody was trigger-happy. I got down low and yelled out: "Don't shoot, godammit. I lost my way to the shithouse."

"I did the same thing last night myself," the guard replied.

I gave him the password and it took another thirty minutes to find my tent and fall onto my cot. It was a two hour round trip. From then on, I used a flashlight. To hell with the Luftwaffe or any German snipers that happened to be around. Our own guards were a greater threat than any Germans.

A few days later, Morelli and I decided to go on sick call. We had had enough with our intestines. We also were aware how dangerous it was to go to the infirmary. We had heard many horror stories from many of the men.

The sergeant there looked annoyed.

"What do you guys want?"

"We ate some bad food on the ship coming over here and we've had diarrhea off and on ever since," I said.

"Wait here and I'll see if I can pry the major loose from his latest copy of Esquire," the sergeant said.

A few minutes later, a sour-looking officer came out. He had a long, hooked nose that could have opened a clam without any difficulty.

"Food poisoning, huh" he grunted. "Diarrhea, huh." Another grunt. "The navy, huh. It wasn't their beans, was it?" Two more grunts followed.

"I don't think so, sir," Morelli said.

"Well, boys, I've heard about all the excuses you guys can think of and I have just the thing for both of you. This will cure you of everything except the clap which you haven't had time to get yet. You take this medicine and I guarantee you won't miss any of the fun your outfit has scheduled for you with the Germans."

I couldn't see how his own mother could like this son-of-a-bitch.

He went to a cabinet and handed each of us a bottle of a clear, thick liquid.

"Take six tablespoons of this as soon as you get back to your tents," the major said, "the whole bottle."

No examination, nothing else. He was obviously a great diagnostician. Just two more malingerers, he must have thought, trying to get out of duty.

We heard the major and the sergeant both laughing as Morelli and I left the tent.

"I don't trust that bastard," I said. "I don't think I'll take his medicine."

"He's a doctor, isn't he?" Morelli said. "The medicine obviously won't kill us and it just might help."

He talked me into it. As soon as we got to our own tent, we took the vile-tasting crap. We should have followed our basic instincts for self-preservation. Five hours later we were both in mortal agony, rolling on the ground next to the latrine, begging for somebody to take mercy on us and end our misery.

That lasted four hours, leaving us dehydrated like two prunes.

"I believe that doctor thinks he can cure the runs by treating us with cholera," I said.

Morelli just rolled his eyes and groaned.

Three days later when we had recovered enough to walk, we found out by checking with the infirmary sergeant that the doctor had given us castor oil, a purgative.

"You'll never find that treatment in the medical books," the sergeant said. "If you survive his treatment, that proves you're strong and healthy."

After one of those treatments, a soldier learns quickly that being in combat against the Germans was a lot safer than being treated by a sadistic old bastard like that.

That's when Morelli decided to get back at old "Hook-Nose". Vengeance was in his heart. And as things would happen, an opportunity presented itself a few days later when Morelli and I were both on KP duty together.

We were in the kitchen tent at 4:30 in the morning at Sgt. Colombresi's kind invitation. We were both surprised to see our dear friend, old Hook-Nose himself, walk in, apparently getting an early start for some reason.

It was pitch-black outside and no lights were allowed. The guards were maniacal about that regulation and were constantly threatening to shoot out any lights they saw. Everybody, including those exalted individuals, the officers, had to empty their own garbage in the sump hole outside the tent in total darkness.

"How many paces to the garbage sump, soldier?" the major inquired, after eating his scrambled eggs, sitting there picking his teeth and belching loudly several times.

The cook was busy at the far end of the tent, so Morelli sang out loud and clear: "Twenty-five, sir."

He knew that it was only fifteen.

About one minute later, we heard some wild cursing and yelling outside the tent that would have gladdened the heart of any infantry-man. Morelli ducked out the front of the tent. I grabbed a broom and a flashlight and went out the back way in the direction of all that cursing.

There was old Hook-Nose, up to his armpits in the garbage sump trying desperately to climb out, only to keep slipping back in again.

"Where is that fucking soldier?" the major screamed hysteri-cally. "I'll have his ass up for a court-martial so fast, his fucking head will spin."

"Why, sir?" I said, extending the broom to him so he could pull himself out. "He distinctly said fifteen paces and it is definitely, if not exactly, or somewhere around fifteen."

"Go fuck yourself, soldier," the major said. He was certainly

22

working himself up to an ugly mood, and so early in the morning. It was a shame to start the day that way.

"Yes sir," I said. "As soon as I get off duty, sir."

"Are you trying to be funny, soldier?"

By this time, I was holding my nose tightly pinched between my thumb and index finger because the major stank worse than anything I've ever smelled on this earth. This made my voice sound odd.

"Absolutely not, sir," I said, exaggerating the odd nasal sound somewhat.

The mess sergeant and the rest of the GIs in the tent had come out by then, all of them holding their noses. Apparently, some of the other guys had received the good major's cholera treatment that couldn't be found in any medical textbook.

"Is that you, Major Wilson?" the mess sergeant asked, his voice sounding much more grotesque than mine. "Dear me, dear me. What an awful stink you've made stirring up all that garbage. Here, let me take that piece of cabbage off your nose. It makes your nose look like a baited hook. And that potato skin in your left ear. Can you hear me all right? Isn't that a shame? I just bet that your pockets are full of all kinds of miserable things. You can take the broom with you, sir, since it's covered with garbage, too."

"You know what you can do with that broom, Sergeant," Major Wilson said.

He walked away muttering under his breath, still cursing, stopping every few steps to shake a leg and empty a pocket.

We never did see Major Wilson in our mess tent after that episode.

A guard finally warned us to close the flap of the tent. By then, if there had been any Luftwaffe around, we would certainly have been bombed.

Morelli had been hiding in the darkness on the far side of the tent, barely able to prevent himself from laughing out loud as he listened to the whole affair.

He pinched his nose and said, "Dear me, dear me. What an awful stink you've made, Major Wilson."

We then proceeded to laugh ourselves silly.

But vengeance burned fiercely in Morelli's heart and he still

23

wasn't satisfied. Two days later, he and I were on latrine duty together. Morelli was assigned to the officer's crap house and I was captain of the day for our own. Again, this was at the kind invitation of our beloved first sergeant, Sgt. Colombresi, who vowed to mold us into top-notch soldiers by giving us extra duty as often as possible.

The army method of keeping a latrine in good order was to throw straw into the hole on which the eight seater rested, then toss a measured amount of gasoline on top of the straw, followed by a lighted match. This method, or some variation thereof, was perfected either during or shortly after the Civil War and was brought to its highest level of execution during World War II. I had become particularly adept at this method simply because I had this kind of extra duty so often. There were many times that I was consulted by a neophyte on latrine duty about the exact mixture of straw and gasoline required for a specific size of latrine. Of course, I always offered my advice without any thought of compensation. Just the right amount of straw, just the right amount of gasoline and, of course, just one lighted match tossed in after a brief interval and voilà, a glorious poof!

Unfortunately, Morelli, not having been on latrine duty as often as I, did not possess the necessary expertise to produce a well-controlled poof. He was unaware that you mustn't wait too long after you pour the gasoline in, because of the volatility of the fuel. I believe he waited for the good major to show up. Unfortunately, Major Wilson did not make his usual trip to the latrine that morning, probably because of constipation and loss of appetite as a consequence of his garbage sump initiation.

So Morelli, standing there and waiting twenty minutes after tossing in the gasoline, finally gave up his dream of a showdown with Major Wilson. He tossed in a match and started toward the entrance.

I had completed my work and was looking toward the officers' latrine, contemplating its perfect blending of form and function.

Suddenly, I saw the whole damned thing rise in the air silently as if pulled by some giant invisible hand, followed by this magnificent explosion that sounded like a 155mm howitzer. Morelli scrambled out on all fours, poking out from underneath the side wall of the tent, nose first. As he ran, he gradually rose to his feet, his legs going like pistons. The whole latrine appeared to be suspended in the air for a moment. It then collapsed, sacred officer excrement flying in all directions. Like a well-trained soldier, I hit the ground and just lay there, watching the whole thing with great admiration. Morelli finally reached me, a hundred-yard dash completed in excellent time, breathing hard. His hair, eyebrows, and clothes were singed from the fire. He was deaf as a door knob from the blast and decorated with excrement.

He had only two words for all future generations to remember: "Holy shit."

I held my nose with two fingers and said, "Morelli, you stink worse than Major Wilson."

Having escaped with his life, vengeance left Morelli. Sgt. Colombresi, revealing an unusual streak of wisdom, never put him on latrine duty again.

****

We waited in the hot sun for about two hours, one single clip of ammo inserted in the breech of our M1s, safety on, tense, alert, edgy, listening to some mortar fire not too far in the distance. An occasional 88 shell swooshed over our heads, the Germans letting us know they were still there.

Stulek finally came back with the directions to our OP. He appeared very excited, speaking rapidly, hands darting back and forth, feet moving in all directions.

"Are you nervous or what, Corporal Stulek?" Brawley asked. "Can't you stand still?"

"I want to show you where our OP is located before dark, so let's get going," Stulek said, his hands moving constantly, first rubbing his nose, then twisting his little finger in his right ear. He shifted his rifle in his left hand, scratched his ass, adjusted his balls, and finally spit into the road.

"We've got plenty of time," Brawley said. "Lets not rush this thing and screw it up."

Our platoon moved out, five jeeps and twenty men. Stulek's jeep was in the lead. We drove into the sun-drenched countryside of Bitche, hearts pounding, scared and tense. This was our first day on the front lines. We feared the worst, but hoped for the best. Thank God we hit a fairly inactive sector of the Western Front, just west of the Maginot and Siegfried Lines. Otherwise, this could have ended up as our last day on the earth.

I was in the last jeep with Sgt. Brawley. Morelli was driving the jeep in front of us. We had gone just a few miles, turning onto a rutted dirt road, the dust ballooning into the air and then coming down slowly. It was already getting much warmer. We could see Stulek's jeep up ahead, following the road that snaked out in broad curves over relatively flat territory, with only an occasional tree to break the monotony. Stulek finally pulled over to the side. We followed and walked over to him.

Everything was disturbingly quiet.

"See that curve in the road ahead?" Stulek said, pointing to a right angle turn in the road.

He still looked agitated. The sun was high in the sky and felt hot on the backs of our necks. I felt uneasy. It was too damned quiet.

"That's the only spot on this road that the Germans have zeroed in with their mortars. You can see the craters scattered on both sides of the road."

He shaded his eyes against the sun as he turned to look at us.

"Periodically, they lob a few mortars into that curve just for the hell of it, using it for target practice, I guess," he continued. "I'll go first, then at varying intervals, the other jeeps will follow. The time intervals have to be different, otherwise the Germans can anticipate our next move and lob one over to meet you as you round that curve. We'll wait for the whole platoon to join together about a half-mile up the road. Don't stop on the road unless you want to be out of this war suddenly and permanently and buried here with all those other poor bastards from World War I.

He jumped back into his jeep and pointed straight up the road, a worried look on his face as his jeep suddenly jerked ahead. His driver didn't waste time. He changed gears quickly and smoothly, and practically flew around that curve. We saw him stop half a mile or so up the road just as he said he would. He waved us on.

"That was easy," Brawley said.

Just then a mortar shell landed a few feet off the curve and we all hit the dirt.

"Oh yeah," Morelli said sarcastically, "that was real easy."

Sgt. Brawley gave him the eye, his lower lip sticking out a mile. He pointed to the next jeep and said, "Go."

The second jeep had no problem. Finally four jeeps had departed and made it safely around that curve. Brawley looked at his watch, waited for another minute, and then looked up.

"What are we waiting for?" he said. "Move out."

Just as we approached the curve, a mortar shell dropped in ahead of our jeep, the blast shaking the hell out of us and pelting us with a rain of gravel. Groves, one of the men in our jeep, calmly took off his helmet and used it as a shield to cover his genitals.

"Keep moving," Brawley yelled out, "or the next one will be right on top of us."

Our driver had slowed down just in time or we would have had that mortar down our throats. When Brawley yelled out, the driver let the clutch out suddenly and we lurched forward, picking up speed quickly as the engine roared. The smell of the explosion was thick in the air. Another shell blasted behind us about fifty yards but we were going at a fast clip by then. Groves had replaced his helmet on his head so I knew we were finally safe.

We stopped behind the other jeeps.

"That was close," Stulek said. "You guys did real well."

"Those fucking bastards," Brawley said. "Come on, let's get the hell out of here."

Morelli looked at me smiling, giving me the thumbs-up sign.

"You're one lucky son-of-a-bitch, Zeb," he said.

I smiled back with a big sigh of relief.

"We're all lucky sons-of-bitches," I said. "Remember where we are: Bitche, France."

We all felt a little better after getting through our first dangerous action. And if we hadn't realized it before, we certainly realized it then. Those bastards were really trying to kill us and we had to be on guard constantly.

We drove on for a few more kilometers, past a cluster of abandoned cement houses, until we came to several large coils of barbed wire lying across the road. We stopped and walked over to Stulek.

"Get that barbed wire off the road," Stulek said to nobody in particular.

"Hold it," a voice called out from the side of the road. A GI came out from behind some bushes and walked over to us slowly. He was holding his M1 on the ready. There was a 100th Division patch on his left shoulder.

"What in Christ's name do you think you're doing?" he said.

"We're going to get that barbed wire off the road and continue up to our OP," Stulek said.

"No, you're not," the GI said. "You guys with the 71st?"

To confuse the Germans about which division was on the line, we weren't wearing our division patches. This appeared to confuse the Americans more than the Germans.

"Yeah," we answered in a chorus.

"My sergeant said there would be some confused 71st Division GIs wandering around here who would probably get their asses shot off the first day they were on the front unless we stationed a man right here. He was right and you can thank him for that. Your OP is about a half-mile back down this road, the beat-up white house, the last one in the bunch on this side. It's the one with the open john in the back with a black umbrella on it so you can feel like King George when you're taking a dump. If you went past this barbed wire, you'd be at the beginning of the German lines about one thousand yards from here and they have a nice little machine gun nest right there to greet new troops like you."

Brawley was the only one to put our feelings into words.

"Godammit, Stulek," he said, "if this GI hadn't been stationed here, we'd all be dead right this minute."

Stulek didn't say a word. He went back to his jeep.

I looked at Morelli. I felt like yelling out at the top of my voice, "Morelli, let's go back. This is all a big mistake. We don't want to play war any longer. These bastards are so stupid, they're going to get us killed our first day on the front."

We got into the jeeps and drove back to the house the GI had described. There was the open john in the back in plain view, set on a slight rise with a black umbrella standing guard to protect the sitter from the sun if not mortar fire and machine gun bullets. King George would have been proud to ascend that throne. It was pure luxury in the middle of a wasteland. How the hell could Stulek have missed it?

We spent two weeks at that OP. There was an awful stink near the house the first night we were there. Morelli and Doyle poked around the next morning and found the partially decomposed body of a German soldier next to the foundation. It was covered over with a few inches of dirt. We had been warned about booby-trapped bodies. They very carefully tied a rope around one of the ankles and started to pull. The whole leg came off. They then tied a rope around the chest and managed to pull the body far enough away so it wouldn't stink up the house. We couldn't understand how the 100th Division tolerated that stench. Perhaps the fear of it being booby-trapped was enough to persuade them to leave it alone.

The only action that took place on this section of the front occurred at night when our infantry patrols were sent out to probe the enemy lines. German patrols would be engaged in a similar action. We'd hear the high-pitched, rapid ratta-tattat of their machine guns and the answering low-pitched, slower beat of our own. There would be sporadic swooshing of artillery passing both ways overhead that we soon learned to ignore.

During the first full day after relieving the 100th Division, our units did some heavy shelling and the Germans responded in a similar fashion, sort of a welcoming salute to the 71st. They were especially hard on A Company positions, lobbing over three hundred shells on the wooden areas in one night. There was very little damage. It was more like an act of intimidation, a flexing of their military muscle.

We were deep in the Alsace-Lorraine region, the same area Americans had fought in during World War I, and it was similar warfare, with both sides fighting from fixed entrenched positions.

There was only sporadic rifle fire and the occasional blast of an exploding Schu mine as some poor son-of-a-bitch accidentally stepped on one, getting his foot blown off in the blackness of the night.

The engineers would lay out markers indicating safe paths through the mine fields. The Germans would rearrange the markers the next day. It was a deadly game. In the dark it was difficult to distinguish one person from another and some of our own men fired upon each other.

The first night the line companies were in their trenches, one stupid second lieutenant, a ninety-day wonder playing at war, crept up silently on the man on guard duty, just like he used to at Fort Benning, trying to catch the poor slob napping. At the first sound the guard heard, he didn't follow the ritual that he had learned in basic training. He didn't yell out, "Halt! Who goes there?" This would have identified his location. He was nervous that first night, fearing that some German would sneak up on him and slit his throat just like he had seen in the movies. So, he merely fired in the direction of the sound. The next morning they found the lieutenant with a bullet hole in his head.

We could never understand the reasoning behind patrols being sent out in the dead of the night. Men on both sides were killed and mutilated while gathering information that was utterly useless.

During our two-week stay in Bitche, we were officially part of the 7th Army, basically fighting on a stationary front. The American Expeditionary Force fought a similar battle in 1917-18. Thank God our military geniuses had given up on the idea of massive frontal assaults in the face of fierce machine gun and artillery fire that simply wiped out entire units without any chance of success. We had heard about the slaughter that took place when our American infantrymen crossed the Rapido River in Italy against overwhelming German forces, suffering stupendous and inexcusable casualties.

That certainly didn't bolster our confidence in any way. Neither did it help us to know that the American 30th Division had been strafed by the 9th U.S. Air Force so many times it was disgraceful. One of the worst episodes occurred during the Battle of the Bulge when the 9th mistakenly bombed Malmedy for three consecutive days even though the town was held by our own 30th Division troops. After that, the 9th U.S. Air Force was known as the American Luftwaffe.

A few days after the 71st took over the positions of the 100th Division, the antitank company that was attached to our 66th Infantry Regiment, while setting up a 57mm gun, was strafed by what appeared to be four of our own P-47s. Three of the men were wounded and two were killed outright. We found out later the planes were piloted by Germans. Our own P-38s were alerted and the Germans were quickly blasted out of the heavens when they made a return visit in another strafing attempt.

We learned not to take anything for granted and to view everything with suspicion.

At the end of that two-week period, we awoke one morning with the order to move out. The Germans had disappeared during the night and we no longer had any enemy troops to observe from our OP.

Our 71st Division was then transferred to the 3rd Army under General Patton, old "Blood and Guts" (our blood and his guts), and the big chase was on.

Chapter 3

Tanks

What Napoleon had written about war was correct: "God is on the side with the most cannon." In Patton's case, it was tanks, not artillery.

At first, we looked at the tankers with great envy. After all, they advanced into battle inside a thirty-two ton monster, protected by thick armor that caused bullets to bounce off like popcorn in a popper. But after listening to some of their harrowing experiences, we preferred to take our chances on foot instead of being incinerated inside a tin can.

It was around Regensburg that the tanks finally caught up to us. We had been reconnoitering behind enemy lines without any chance of support from our armored divisions. The lack of gasoline was the problem. The tanks were real gas guzzlers.

"The tanks will be catching up to us this afternoon," Brawley said, "and I need one man to direct them to designated areas when they get here. Zebrowski, you come with me."

At least this isn't latrine duty, I thought.

Brawley and I drove out into the country about four or five miles on a dirt road, snaking through farm land and woods that appeared totally deserted.

"Are you sure that this area is in our hands, Sergeant?" I asked Brawley.

"Godammit, it better be," Brawley answered. "Lieut. Rickey is the one who gave me these orders."

"Kaputt?" I said, surprised.

"Kaputt, himself," he said.

"Then you know something has to go wrong," I said.

We had renamed our lieutenant, "Kaputt," a name he'd accepted without complaining.

"Do you know what happened to Densman in the wire section?" I asked Brawley.

"No," he said. "What happened to him?"

"Well, you know their exalted leader, Capt. Mudger, is just like our lieutenant. They both don't know how to read a map. Both of them have two left feet and two left hands. It's amazing that they can even dress themselves without help. And it's even a greater miracle that we're all still alive."

"What happened to Densman?"

"Mudger told Densman to take a wire team and string wire to a little village that Densman was pretty sure was still in German hands. 'But Captain, I know for a fact that that town is still in German hands,' Densman told Mudger. Do you think the captain listened to Densman? 'No, it isn't,' Mudger retorted. He wasn't going to listen to a mere sergeant. 'Our troops took that town last night,' Mudger said. 'Now take three men and string wire to that point and don't argue with me.' Well, that's what Densman did. He strung wire to a town still held by the Germans. Anterhaus was shot in the left arm, Enriquez was hit in the right arm and back, and Kelley was hit by 88 shrapnel that castrated him, according to the last report we got. Densman, by some miracle, wasn't hit, probably because he didn't make a run for it, having decided it was useless. They were all captured, of course, and Densman had to bandage up all their wounds. He escaped a week later and made his way back to the company area through the enemy lines."

"Well," Brawley said, "that's not going to happen this time. According to the information Kaputt gave me, they'll be coming down this road, Zebrowski, and I want you to direct them into these fields next to the road."

Brawley had a map in his left hand. He was pointing to the various fields that looked solid enough to hold the tanks.

"Are you sure they'll be coming from this direction?" I asked.

"According to Mudger, I mean Kaputt, that's the road. I can

only tell you what I've been told myself."

"Why couldn't you just put up a sign at that point? They can see those fields just as well as I can. And furthermore, why couldn't you send another man out here with me? The rest of the platoon is just pillaging the houses in that village. Didn't you ever hear of the buddy system?"

"One man's enough for this job," Brawley said. "After all, you're only going to direct some tank traffic and you won't be here that long. Quit bitching."

"I hope they're American Shermans I direct and not German Tigers or Panthers," I said.

Brawley looked at his watch.

"It's one o'clock now and we expect them to start arriving around four," Brawley said. "It'll take about two or three hours for them to group here and I'll be back to pick you up at nine."

"At nine?" I protested. "Why so late?"

"They may take longer to get here and they won't all get here at once," Brawley said. "Don't stay out in the open in case there are any stray German soldiers wandering around looking for an easy target."

He got back into the jeep.

"Any other encouraging advice, Sergeant?"

"I agree with you," he said.

"What do you mean, about Mudger and Kaputt?"

"No," he said. "I hope they're Shermans that come down that road and not Tigers and Panthers."

He waved at me as he gunned the motor and pulled away.

Another good friend of mine, I thought, just like Sgt. Colombresi. I started to look around. I was all alone in the middle of nowhere. I didn't even know the name of the town where our platoon was quartered for the night.

I took off into the woods. I found some pine branches lying around that had been knocked down by the wind and made a small unobtrusive shelter for myself. I had a good view of the intersection and the road the tanks were supposed to come down, but not a clear view to the rear.

"I hope they're Shermans and not Tigers or Panthers," Sgt.

Brawley had said, the son-of-a-bitch. That was certainly a comforting thought. And he had gotten the orders from Lieut. Rickey, Kaputt himself, who couldn't read a road map of Scitico, Connecticut, population five hundred.

I spent the next three hours checking the area and getting into and out of my shelter. I did it often enough so that I could sneak in and out quickly if I had to.

About four o'clock, I heard a rumbling sound coming from the road Brawley had pointed out to me. It got louder and louder until the ground seemed to vibrate. I was in my shelter, heart pounding. That fucking Brawley. The first tank finally came clanking down, tracks rattling and squealing. It was a Sherman, a glorious sight. I ran out with a big smile and pointed to the field on my left. The tanker gunned the engine as if to say "Hello," and then made a sharp ninety degree turn, churning up the road in a hail of gravel. One after another they came, big clanking monsters, hundreds of them. By six o'clock, all of them were shut down for the night and everything had quieted down.

Infantrymen were always glad to see the tankers, and the tankers were always happy to coordinate their actions with the infantry. When people think of Patton, they think of tanks, and it is a fact that Patton scored many of his greatest feats with tanks. But the truth of the matter was that the greatest achievements were realized when the tanks supported the infantry and not the other way around.

One day, our platoon had come across about one hundred tanks holed up in a little town on the approaches to Bayreuth. It was April 14, 1945. The tankers had gotten a good distance ahead of us, but on this day they were held up by strong antitank defenses that the Germans had mounted to slow down Patton.

A colonel was poring over maps with his officers in the center of the town when Kaputt went up to him. The colonel looked up from his maps impatiently, puffed on his cigar, and then growled, "What can I do for you, Lieutenant?"

Kaputt cleared his throat and appeared to have a hard time getting started.

"I've got orders from S2 to reconnoiter up ahead for another five kilometers, sir, and I'd like to know if there is any significant German resistance there."

"Well, Lieutenant," the colonel said, pushing back his helmet, puffing several times on his cigar, then taking it out of his mouth and closely examining the chewed end, "I've been stuck here for three days because of the German forces up ahead and I've already lost ten tanks. But if you have your heart set on going in that direction, I'll be glad to give you three tanks as an escort and you can try."

We looked at Kaputt as his poor old brain tried to figure out the ramifications of that singular offer.

"If we go up that road, Morelli," I whispered, "that will be the end of the road for us."

"We all know that Kaputt is dumb," Morelli said, "but he can't be that dumb. Anyway, I believe the colonel is leading him on. He can't be serious."

Kaputt stood there in the middle of the road, thinking.

"Well, Lieutenant, what is your decision?" the colonel prompted him.

Kaputt rubbed his jaw and looked up the road.

"I'd better speak to S2 before I accept your offer, Colonel," he said.

"I believe that's a wise move, Lieutenant," the colonel said.

He turned back to his maps.

On the radio we could hear Major Booker nearly go into hysterics.

"What?" he screamed. "Are you out of your mind, Lieutenant? The colonel was going to give you three tanks as an escort? He must have been pulling your leg. Get back to headquarters with your men immediately before you do something stupid. Do not, I say again, do not go up that road under any circumstances."

The line companies were called up to penetrate the enemy's defenses and in twenty-four hours, the area was cleaned out and the tanks continued on their majestic drive against the fleeing Germans.

Early in World War II, it seemed that the officers commanding the armored units still had a cavalry complex and would order attacks in fierce, frontal assaults just like the infantry was trained to do in World War I. This was evident in Africa, especially against poorly equipped Italian troops, who were not prepared for all-out tank assaults and would turn-tail and head for the rear as fast as they could go. The tankers began to think of themselves as invincible. That is until they met the Germans, who were equipped with the deadly 88, the best big gun to come out of World War II. They also had panzerfausts that could disable a tank with one blast, leaving it an ignited tin can.

Tank commanders, after some disastrous encounters with the Germans, quickly realized that for a tank assault to be successful, the infantry was necessary to knock out the antitank defenses of the enemy. This was especially apparent in Normandy, where the berms and hedgerows made it difficult for tanks to make any significant progress. The Germans hid from the tanks until the very last moment and then let loose with a panzerfaust (a one-shot bazooka that looked like a stove pipe with a large metal bulb on one end).

It was true that when the Germans were in total disarray, the tankers made their greatest penetrations through enemy territory, often only limited by their own supply lines. But against entrenched and well-equipped and well-defended units, the tanks were best used as slow metal monsters that lay waiting while the infantry cleared the area of enemy troops.

I walked down to the field where the first tanks had entered. Most of the guys were stretched out on the ground resting.

"Am I glad to see you guys," I said.

"It's nice to be back with the infantry again," one of the tankers said. "We had a little trouble getting gas, you know, so you guys got ahead of us."

"I always thought I'd prefer to be a tanker than an infantryman," I said.

"And we always thought it would be a helluva lot nicer being an infantryman instead of a tanker," another tanker interjected.

"Yeah, especially when you learn in combat that every time a Sherman gets hit, it bursts into flames," another tanker said.

"And you have exactly three seconds to get out," another popped up,

"That means only the commander has a chance to get out. The rest of the crew is incinerated. When a Sherman gets hit, the armor turns a bright red like a flaming sunset. It's the last sunset a tanker sees."

"Jesus Christ," I said. "You guys don't paint a pretty picture. You're making me damn glad I'm an infantryman."

"A Churchill isn't as bad as a Sherman," the first tanker said. "It only bursts into flames sixty percent of the time with a direct hit and you have a little more time to get out, a total of ten seconds."

"How does a Sherman stack up against a Tiger or a Panther?" I asked.

"Don't ask, because you'll be sorry you did," another tanker yelled out. "See that cannon on the Sherman? That's a 75mm, which has no frontal penetration of a German Tiger or Panther. The Panther however, has no problem penetrating the frontal armor of a Sherman at three thousand yards."

I whistled in amazement.

"We have to get within six hundred yards to penetrate the front of a Panther turret and three hundred yards for a Tiger. And do you think they'll let us sneak up on them like that? The Tiger can penetrate the Sherman turret at eighteen hundred yards and the Panther can do the same at three thousand yards. Now do you know why we like the infantry to be with us at all times?"

"You can bet your ass I'll never ask for a transfer to a tank outfit," I said.

Another tanker popped into the conversation.

"Thank God the Germans are retreating because when they turn around to fight they're real tough bastards."

It was getting dark and I didn't want to miss Brawley if he decided to come early so I went back to the road. By seven o'clock, everybody was asleep except for the guards they had posted. I went into the woods and sat down. Everybody thinks that men in other units always have it easier, but after listening to the tankers I came to the conclusion that being in the infantry wasn't so bad, especially if you didn't have to put up with sergeants like Colombresi and Brawley.

Nine o'clock came and went.

I bet that son-of-a-bitch isn't coming, I thought, looking at the luminescent dial of my GI Bulova. What the hell does he care if one of his men is missing?

It was totally black. I couldn't see a foot in front of my face.

Ten o'clock came and went.

Now, I asked myself, what the hell is the goddamned army regulation regarding maintaining your post? Did my duty end at nine when Brawley was supposed to pick me up? Should I start back up that road leading to the village where my platoon was quartered? Was Brawley killed by some German soldier while he was on his way to pick me up? And if so, perhaps no one else knows that I'm stuck out here in the darkness of the night. And if that son-of-a-bitch is still alive, would he say that I deserted my post if I started to walk back?

By eleven o'clock, I was real edgy, still thinking that somebody might sneak up on me and slit my throat. But it was so dark that I felt moderately relieved. After all, if I couldn't see them, then they couldn't see me, either.

I was totally disgusted with Sam Brawley. There he is, the bastard, in his nice warm fart sack, belly full, sound asleep, not caring one whit for one of his men missing all night.

I started back. To hell with Sam Brawley and all the rest of those bastards in my platoon. How could they go to sleep knowing one of their men was gone, God knows where? Why didn't they at least make an attempt at a search of some kind?

As I walked up the road, making as little noise as possible and having great difficulty staying in the center of the road because of the darkness, I stopped periodically to listen, while holding my breath. I heard sounds coming from the woods, a twig snapping here and there, a branch bending and whipping back. I hurried on and then stopped again, wondering if it was my imagination. No, there it was again, without a doubt. Germans were slipping through the woods. Were they civilians or soldiers? Were they going west to avoid being captured by the Russians or were they going to infiltrate the village and set up some kind of counterattack?

I walked for about an hour.

"Who's that out there?" a nervous voice yelled out suddenly. "Speak up or I'll shoot."

I nearly jumped a mile. I hadn't realized I had reached the village.

"Don't shoot," I yelled back. "Tommy."

"Dorsey," the voice said. "What the hell are you doing out here at this time of the night?"

I explained my situation.

"Nice guys in your platoon," he said.

"Do you happen to know where the I and R Platoon is quartered?" I asked.

"About the third house up on the right, but I'm not sure."

He was wrong.

I entered three houses of sleeping men, falling all over them lying on the floor before I recognized Morelli's voice as I stumbled over his legs.

"Where the hell have you been?" he whispered. "I thought for sure some German got you."

"Never mind that," I said. "Where's Brawley sleeping?"

"He's just inside the next room, first one on the left."

I stepped over several other men in their sleeping bags. As I entered the next room, I gave a good swing with my right boot and deliberately fell on top of the man snoring there, crashing down on him rifle and all.

"Ouch, godammit," Brawley yelled out.

I grabbed my helmet and swung it in a wide arc just above the floor until I felt it connect with Sam Brawley's body.

"You son-of-a-bitch," Brawley roared out. "What the hell do you think you're doing?"

"Oh, is that you, Sgt. Brawley?" I said in mock surprise. "I'm sorry I woke you up."

"Is that you, Zebrowski?" Brawley said.

"Yeah, it's me," I answered.

"I forgot to pick you up," he said, yawning.

"Go piss up a tree, Sergeant," I said.

"Go to sleep, Zebrowski. I'll talk to you about it in the morning. Jesus Christ, you whacked the shit out of me."

"Go to sleep, Sergeant. I believe we're finished talking."

Brawley grunted and farted. I went to sleep, tired, mad, and hungry.

Brawley never said another word about it in the morning.

Chapter 4

Basic Training

After Ba-ba-balls Loudry, my best friend and the spit-ball king of the world, joined the army in September, 1944, our hometown was dead. Two of my brothers had joined and most of my friends were in the service. High school was no challenge. In fact, it was boring and my life seemed to have entered a state of suspended animation. I was like a person in a trance, going through the motions of living, but actually uninvolved.

By mid-February, I was practically a basket case, just moping around. I went to see Harry Bagosian, our high school principal, a short, fat, baggy-pants Armenian. He was just about the worst teacher at Enfield High School, so he was awarded the job of principal. He liked to be called Harry to show he was one of the boys.

"Harry," I said, "I'd like to join the army."

He was sitting at his desk, looking at me above the bags hanging beneath his eyes. He put down the newspaper he had been reading.

"Well, Mr. Zebrowski," he said, stifling a yawn, "why don't you? Everybody else seems to be doing the same thing."

"But I'm only half-way through my senior year, Harry," I said.

"That's true," he said. "But you can wait until the end of the school year. That's only four months away. That'll solve your problem."

"I don't want to wait until June," I said.

"Well, you can quit now," he said. "Nobody's stopping you. But wouldn't that be foolish?"

"When I get out of the service," I said, "I plan to go to Dartmouth College, where my brother, Stan, went. I don't want to face the problem of repeating my senior year of high school. I'm bored to death with high school as it is."

"Are you proposing, Mr. Zebrowski, that I let you graduate with your class in absentia in June even though you plan to quit now?" he said, somewhat startled.

"Exactly," I said.

"Mrs. Malley," he yelled out to his secretary, the person who really ran the school. "Get me Mr. Zebrowski's transcript, please."

Harry was not one to move out of his chair if he didn't have to. He already knew what was in the transcript because I had the highest average in my class.

He looked at the transcript for a few minutes, his eyes like two brown marbles half-hidden behind his saggy bags. He finally stood up and extended his right hand.

"It's a deal, Mr. Zebrowski," he said. "You can quit now and join the army and I promise you that you'll get your diploma in June."

"Thanks, Harry," I said, shaking his limp hand.

"And Mr. Zebrowski," he said, with both hands on his hips.

"Yes?"

"Promise me you won't get your ass shot off," he said, smiling. "The recruiters tell me there's nothing left open in the army except the infantry and I'd have a hard time thinking of you as a rifle-toting foot soldier."

Two weeks later, I got on the train at Windsor Locks, Connecticut, the youngest of a brood of ten, off to war. On the train I had a disturbing thought. What if Harry Bagosian suddenly decided to drop dead from excessive inactivity? I had nothing on paper to verify the deal we had made in the confines of his office and I'd have to go through my senior year all over again. Well, it was too late to worry about it now.

At Fort Devens, Massachusetts, I took that one step forward, swearing allegiance to my country, and was then considered a member of the U.S. Armed Forces, a one hundred twenty-five pound fighting demon.

That first night in camp, I was given immediate recognition in the army, being appointed Fire Marshal. This meant that I stoked the furnaces and tended to them all night while everybody else slept.

"You have to bank these furnaces just right, piling the coal in the back about twelve inches, and then grading downward gradually to the furnace door," my sergeant instructor advised me, giving me the benefit of his years of experience in the regular army.

"Why do you have to do that?" I asked. "Why can't you just shovel in the coal. It's all going to burn, isn't it?"

"If you don't do it the way I tell you, the men in the barracks might be asphyxiated," the sergeant answered.

"Asphyxiated from what," I asked.

"Carbon monoxide," he said, looking annoyed.

"Is there a crack in the burning compartment?" I asked.

I didn't want to be responsible for the death of one hundred men through sheer stupidity.

"How the hell should I know?" the sergeant growled, increasingly irritated by my questioning.

"How does carbon monoxide get into the hot air blown into the barracks where the men are sleeping if there isn't a crack in the burning compartment?" I persisted.

"Look, soldier," he said. "I'm just telling you what I've been told. Don't ask so many questions. This isn't a critical point in the war effort. Anyway, if the men died from carbon monoxide poisoning, they'd turn a bright cherry red. That's how you'd know whether you fucked up or not."

"That's interesting," I said. "Why would they turn cherry red in the presence of carbon monoxide?"

"Jesus Christ," the sergeant exploded. "Are you going to ask questions all night?"

"Don't get mad," I said. "Now I suppose after these minimal instructions, I'm to be considered an expert Fire Marshal? That's great, that's really great."

"You're going to be as much of an expert as I am," the sergeant said. "Remember, you're in the army now."

Where did I hear those words before? Oh yes, Irving Berlin. I was going to hear that phrase many times over the next few years.

That was my first encounter with the military mind. The lesson was: "Don't ask questions, just follow the fucking orders."

That night, after shoveling coal into furnaces in three different buildings, sweating my balls off, I ran up stairs and flashed a light into the faces of the sleeping men to see if they were turning red.

Some of the guys woke up and they were not very polite as they lay there blinking against the bright light shining in their faces.

"What the fuck do you think you're doing?" one of them growled at me as he propped himself up on one elbow.

"I'm making sure you're not turning red and dying from carbon monoxide poisoning, that's what I'm doing," I said. "I'm the Fire Marshal and that's my job."

"Go shovel your fucking coal," he grumbled. "If you shine that light in my eyes again, you won't be the Fire Marshal long."

I ran up and downstairs all night long, making sure that I didn't flash the light on the same guy more than once or I probably would have had a fight on my hands.

No one died.

After many orientation lectures detailing the various ways that the army was planning to reduce all of us to an absolute zero, and viewing on the big screen horrible movies of men suffering from syphilis and gonorrhea and buboes with dongs thirty feet long, always shown before supper, I was shipped out to Fort McClellan, Alabama, for sixteen weeks of basic training.

The same movies we saw at Fort Devens were repeated at Fort McClellan.

The main point of basic training was to convince you that you were nothing but a piece of crap with two arms and two legs that now belonged to the U.S. Army. The legs were for marching and the arms were meant to hold a rifle. Remembering that you had a brain was a detriment to advancement and could create great conflict with your superior officers.

We started with the M1 rifle, firing the weapon on both the regular fixed firing range and the combat range. We spent some time bayoneting straw dummies, being solemnly instructed on the proper way to grunt as we did so. On the fixed firing range, we fired our rifles at distances of one hundred, two hundred, and five hundred yards in the standing, kneeling, and prone positions. On the combat range, we set our sights at three hundred yards, which was considered combat range, and then shot above or below the targets to compensate for the different distances beyond or short of the target.

We got to the combat range the day after a heavy rain storm swamped the area.

Sgt. Farmer stood in front of us, his thumbs hooked into his cartridge belt.

"You've got ten minutes," he barked out gruffly, "to get into your pits before the first group starts firing. Then the first group will replace you in the pits and the second group will have their turn to show us how good they are. Now move out."

He clapped his hands and we ran out into the mud and water. There were twelve targets altogether, and I was assigned to the tenth pit. We were instructed to wave the target side to side if there was no hit and up and down if it had been hit. My pit was down range about three hundred and fifty yards. It had two logs and some gravel built up in front of it and was completely filled with water. I couldn't see bottom.

I looked at my watch. There wasn't enough time to empty the pit or to run back. I took off my helmet and started to bail like a madman. I managed to lower the water level about two feet but water kept running into the pit. I found some hefty branches in the area and laid them across the sides. They were just strong enough to hold me. The pit was eight feet deep and I couldn't swim. Just as I stretched out, the firing began. Nobody hit my target so I did a lot of waving. Most of the bullets hit the dirt and the logs just in front of my head.

I kept remembering what our rifle instructor had told us: "An M1 is capable of penetrating a twelve-inch tree."

That made me feel great. I could hear the water trickling into the pit and it was mighty cold. By the time I was there fifteen minutes, I was covered up to my rear end.

This whole system must have been devised by a bunch of madmen, I thought. We'll never get to see combat because we'll be killed right here in the States.

One of the men in our group wasn't able to bail out his pit fast enough. It was eight feet deep like all the rest with walls built of logs placed one on top of another. He had a precarious perch holding onto the logs in the wall and felt himself slipping. He took off his helmet and put it on top of the pole holding his target. He showed it to me after we got back to the firing line. It had three bullets in it.

After an hour of firing and hearing the bullets whacking into those logs in front of my head, we got out of the pits and took our places on the firing line. The sergeant, his thumbs still hooked in his cartridge belt, laughed at us.

"All you guys look as if you just pissed your pants," he said.

"Ho-ho-ho-ho-ho," one of the guys laughed a fake laugh. Gradually, we all joined in until everybody was laughing a loud artificial Santa Claus laugh.

The sergeant got the message.

When I fired, I deliberately shot to the left of the pits, so that I wouldn't hit any of the men holding the targets. I got a zero for my score. I didn't hit any of the men, either.

Afterward, when we complained to the sergeant about not having enough time to empty the pits, he looked at us surprised and then laughed derisively.

"We gave you ten minutes," he said. "In combat, you don't get any ready time. You just get your head blown off and then nobody has to listen to your boy-scout complaints."

It was useless to try to tell him that this was not combat and he didn't have to jeopardize any of our lives.

While at McClellan, we had several gas-mask drills. We would line up outside a building filled with tear gas. Each man would have to step into the building with his gas mask still unopened in it's own bag. Upon entering, you then put on your gas mask as quickly as you could, blowing out the air that was trapped inside the mask. Then to prove to yourself that the building was loaded with tear gas, we were instructed to remove the masks while still in the building, and then quickly walk outside. This little maneuver certainly proved to everybody's satisfaction that we were in the presence of tear gas, as we tearfully eyed one another. In combat, we threw away our gas masks soon after we hit the front. We used the bag to store personal items.

The only other useful exercise we were exposed to was the infiltration course. This consisted of crawling one hundred yards under direct machine gun fire. Tracers were used to let us see that live ammunition was being used. Every fifth round lit up and you could follow its path.

We crawled under barbed wire and slid on our backs while explosions were triggered in scattered areas around us. That was the only simulated combat we had during basic training.

The rest of the training was taken up by close-order drill and lectures. If the military experts believed this was sufficient training to put a man into combat, they were wrong. We were sheep being led to slaughter.

The first Sunday I was at Fort McClellan, I got up early and started reading a short story by Ernest Hemingway, "The short Happy Life of Francis Macomber". Part way through, I went to the latrine which was completely empty, to sit down, relax, and continue reading. I didn't pay any particular attention to where I sat, picking the last toilet in a row of twelve. These were not divided into separate stalls. That was not the army way. Individual compartments would be for human beings and an infantryman was a far cry from that. I had the whole place to myself and I was engrossed in the story. When I finished, I stood up to pull up my trousers and happened to look at the wall in back of the toilet.

There in plain view was a white sign with bold black letters: "For GU Only." I nearly fainted. Oh my God, I thought to myself, I had used the one toilet in the whole latrine that was reserved for those stupid nuts who had syphilis and gonorrhea.

I rushed over to the orderly room, my mind filled with images of thirty foot cocks with horrible chancres and oozing pus, just like in the movies that we were continually forced to see.

Corporal Mather was busy at the desk, working on some papers. He was from Texas and had always been decent to all of the men in the short time we had been there.

"Corporal, I have to speak to you immediately," I said, trying to conceal my panic. I was practically hysterical with worry, being victimized by a great imagination.

"Now calm down, Zebrowski," he said. "What's troubling you? Did you get some bad news from home?"

"I just sat on a toilet in the latrine marked 'For GU Only,'" I said. "Should I go to the infirmary?"

Corporal Mather burst out laughing.

"This is no laughing matter, Corporal," I said. "If I'm going to get syphilis or gonorrhea, I would prefer to get it the old fashion way."

"Take it easy, soldier," Corporal Mather said, putting a hand on my shoulder. "Sit down here for a moment."

We sat down. I was sweating bullets.

"First of all," he said, 'you're not going to get syphilis or gonorrhea or buboes or anything else you've seen in those army horror movies. The toilet marked 'For GU Only,' is the cleanest toilet in the latrine. Nobody ever uses it."

"Are you trying to make me feel better, Corporal, or is that really the truth?"

"If you don't believe me," Corporal Mather said, "just keep an eye on that toilet every time you're in the latrine. I'll give you one hundred to one odds that you'll never see anybody sitting on that john."

As I left the orderly room, I thought, well, that's making a first-class ass of yourself, buddy.

I did what the corporal suggested and watched the latrine surreptitiously for a week or so. I made sure I visited it when it was very crowded and men had to wait for a seat. Corporal Mather was right. No matter how crowded the latrine was, nobody ever sat on the toilet with the sign, and neither did I. I never took reading material into the latrine after that.

Once a week we had forced field marches with full field packs. We started out with five-mile marches and by the eighth week, we took a twenty-mile hike into the hills of Alabama. The most unusual march we took was up a mountain on a sweltering summer's day. We started out with nine hundred men and were restricted to one canteen of water per man. Undoubtedly, this restriction of water was the result of a committee of brilliant military minds poring over various ways to develop a fighting man. They could not have been just plain sadistic or merely stupid. While we were forced to wear a full field pack, the officers wore a light pack stuffed with toilet paper or some underwear. We carried nine and one-half pound M1s. The officers carried light carbines or .45s in holsters on their cartridge belts. We walked on a never-ending red dirt road that was blazing in the hot summer sun. Heat waves shimmered in the distance. The temperature hovered around 100 degrees and the humidity was terribly high. Up, up, the mountain we went. As we rounded each curve, there was another one up ahead exactly like the one we had just passed. At the beginning of the march, we were allowed ten-minute breaks every hour. Within two hours, all our water was gone. At three hours, our break lasted twenty minutes.

At six hours, our breaks were extended to thirty minutes. This is what hell must be like, I thought.

By the time we had climbed halfway up the mountain, most of the men had dropped out because of heat prostration. I was one of the hundred brave, but stupid souls, who made it to the top. By then, my pulse was racing at one hundred and forty and I was ready to black out. My vision was obscured by a black shroud and my head was spinning.

At the top, we threw our packs down along with our rifles and helmets and stretched out beneath the trees. Nobody moved or made a sound for one solid hour. It had taken us twelve hours to reach the top of that mountain in Alabama and I really think I came very close to dying. None of the officers would take credit for the order to limit the men to one canteen of water.

One day we marched out five miles to hear a lecture on bayoneting the enemy. We were told to stack our rifles, as usual, three in a group. There is a small metal double prong stacking hook on the upper part of the M1 rifle that is used for this purpose. Two other men and I stacked our rifles according to established procedure and as we stepped away the stack collapsed.

For punishment, since that was a grave military crime, the three of us had to stand at attention that evening for one hour in front of the orderly room facing the wall. That certainly didn't teach us to stack our rifles with any greater dexterity. Neither did it teach us to have greater respect for our rifles. It did piss us off, however.

I never had to stack my rifle again after basic training. I believe stacking rifles was a custom preserved from General George Armstrong Custer's day. Three rifles stacked properly had all the appearance of a small teepee, something to remind the cavalry of their ever-present enemy, the Indian.

These nuisances, which we called chickenshit, gradually mounted up until we felt our biggest enemy was the individual officer or noncom who shoved his rank down our throats and, at the same time, derived so much enjoyment out of making us miserable.

I scored high on all the tests the army administered, including the one that tested your ability to discriminate between a series of dits and dahs that we heard through ear phones. My rifle training was terminated after eight weeks and I started to learn how to receive and send Morse code.

The army used a method called "The Greek Chorus System." Out tutor would stand in front of us and go through five or six letters of the alphabet at a time.

"A, didah, A."

We would repeat this, just like a Greek chorus in the ancient Greek plays.

"B, dahdidit, B."

Again we would repeat exactly what our instructor said. "Didah" represented a dot dash and "dahdidit" dash dot dot. That's what it sounded like through the ear phones. We did that for five hours every day for five days. It proved to be a very effective method for teaching the Morse code. At the end of that first week, most of us were capable of receiving seven words a minute, encoded in four letter codes. We then transferred to ear phones. Each hour of listening to code sent at a specific speed was followed by a test that we could take or ignore.

As our proficiency improved and we became more confident, we'd take the test and move on to the next speed if we passed.

We jumped two words a minute with each advancement. At the end of six weeks, I was capable of receiving and sending twenty-two words a minute.

During this time, we were constantly reminded that we were infantrymen first and radiomen second. When we finally got into combat, we never used Morse code. It was all voice transmission. There was no time for Morse code or encoding messages. We didn't care if the Germans were listening or not. We had overwhelming forces and the war was moving rapidly.

After the war was over, we went back to Morse code, which was more fun than simple voice transmission.

The last week of my basic training in July, 1944, we were on bivouac in the hills of Alabama. I was lying in the foxhole that I had just finished digging in the hard rocky clay, fiddling with my FM government-issue radio and scratching my bug bites. It was just past nine o'clock at night when I happened to come across a commercial station from Hartford, Connecticut. It was WTIC. This was a fluke because FM radio waves travel in a straight line. The signal must have bounced off some clouds to reach the hills of Alabama. Abe Lyman and his orchestra were playing their usual Friday night waltzes and for a while, I felt I was back home. It was a great feeling.

The program was suddenly interrupted by a special newscast. They announced the terrible circus fire that had occurred in Hartford that day and the great number of people who had died, many of them children.

War was not the only tragedy on this earth.

Chapter 5

Fort Benning

I completed my basic training, which consisted of eight weeks of infantry training followed by eight weeks of radio communication, and was rewarded, like all the rest of the men, with a two-week furlough. I went back home to Thompsonville, Connecticut, and briefly played the role of the hero. I was instructed to report to Headquarters Company, Fifth Infantry Regiment, Seventy-first Division at Fort Benning, Georgia, having been declared fit to face the enemy. I was seventy-one inches of solid infantryman, one hundred twenty-five pounds of pure bone and muscle, hardened into steel, if you can believe that.

Little did I realize that my first enemy was to be Gaetano Colombresi, first sergeant of Headquarters Company. Colombresi was a skinny little runt with long arms and the intelligent look of an ape. He spoke with an artificially gruff voice. Brought up in the hills of Calabria in southern Italy, and obviously sent by Benito Mussolini as a mole to undermine the morale of the American infantryman, he was ideally suited to make everybody's life miserable.

The company clerk, Corporal Majchack, took my papers and told me to report to the supply sergeant, Sgt. Brook, for my M1 rifle and the rest of my gear. Sgt. Brook took one look at my skinny body and broke out into a demonic laugh.

"Ah," he said, his voice dripping with honey. "Another fighting machine sent to us from our best training grounds, this time Fort McClellan, known for its red clay, its death-defying hill, called Dragass Hill by its graduates, and its fighting men the world over."

Apparently, he had been there himself at one time in his training.

"I have just the weapon for you to administer the coup de grâce to Herr Hitler and his cut-throat gang of murderers."

He was obviously in a wonderful mood, singing "Heigh-ho, heigh-ho, it's off to work we go," as he piled up my gear on the counter.

"Now for the pièce de résistance," he said. "This will demolish the morale of any German soldier that faces you, including the vaunted and feared SS."

Whistling "Yankee Doodle," he went to the far end of the supply room and brought back an M1 that was so rusty I didn't even want to touch it.

"I've been saving this beautiful rifle for just the right man who could really appreciate a vintage weapon like this. As soon as you walked through our humble portals, I instinctively recognized that you were that specific individual truly marked for greatness."

"Where the hell did you get that piece of junk?" I asked.

"This is a special M1, made to look old, in fact ancient, by a unique process called neglect and misuse. It deceives the enemy and gives him a false sense of security. I knew you'd be impressed as soon as you laid your baby blues on it. I had hundreds of men begging me to give them this rifle, but I refused them all. I know you'll love the rear sight. See how it wiggles all over the place. And when you press the clip release, you'll hear the magnificent sound of grinding sand. This will certainly test your ability to clean a rifle. I believe they taught you how to do that at Fort McClellan, but probably not the clip release because that's basically impossible. You'll learn to love this rifle after you spend all your spare time the next few months caressing it back to shape."

"I'm not going to take that rifle, Sergeant," I said.

"Oh, yes you are, soldier," he sang out joyously. "It's the only one we have left. Besides, it's giving me a bad reputation staying here where everybody can see it. Henceforth, dear boy, as they say in the jolly old British Army, it's yours forever, to keep and treasure."

Sgt. Brook was smoking a cigarette and laughing hard, snorting, coughing, gagging, gasping, turning shades of red and then blue, clutching his belly, and finally bending over so far his head was below the counter.

"I'm glad you're having such a good time, Sergeant," I said. "What kind of tobacco are you smoking? And is everybody in this company going to be so happy to see me?"

I took the weapon and the rest of my gear and started toward the door.

"You haven't seen anything yet, soldier," Sgt. Brook croaked out, not having fully recovered from his fit of laughter.

He had a fiendish look on his face.

"At precisely eleven hundred hours this morning," he continued, "Capt. Davis will celebrate your arrival on this very spot on the planet with a white patch inspection of that glorious weapon I just put in your custody. At that time you will also meet our first sergeant, that born leader of men and the army's secret weapon, Sgt. Gaetano Colombresi. I can guarantee that you'll be very impressed with your first encounter with that distinguished descendant of the Neanderthal Man."

I had enough of Sgt. Brook by that time. I went hurriedly to my assigned bunk. All the men had their weapons broken down, busily cleaning away like a bunch of beavers.

Morelli, who had arrived a few weeks before me, was in the next bunk. He introduced himself, took one look at my M1, and then made the sign of the cross.

"Oh, you poor son-of-a-bitch," he said. "Sgt. Brook is at it again. I'll bet you any odds you'll never have that rifle cleaned in two hours."

"Thanks, Morelli," I said. "Thanks a lot."

"And when Sgt. Colombresi takes one look at that worthless piece of junk that Brook gave you, you can kiss your ass good-by," he continued, now smiling broadly.

"Thanks again, Morelli. I appreciate your kind words of encouragement."

Morelli was right. It was impossible to get that piece of junk clean in two hours or even two weeks or months and I was resigned to kiss my ass good-by. The bore was horribly pitted, rusty, and full of filth. It probably would have exploded if fired in that condition. After constant brushing and cleaning with Hoppe's nitro powder solvent and a variety of oils that Morelli and the other men let me try, the white patches still came out black.

"Good-by, Zebrowski," Morelli said in a false tone of sadness. "It was nice knowing you this brief moment in time. Now you're destined to spend the rest of your life on KP."

I could see that I was all set to make a grand impression my first day in Headquarters Company.

At precisely eleven hundred hours, a runty little ape of a man with long arms that seemed to reach the floor, wearing first sergeant's stripes, came into the room, scowling. He yelled out a loud grunting, unrecognizable sound that I assumed was "Attention." Right behind him was Capt. Davis, who bounced in looking very eager and keen to play soldier, obviously hoping to wreck our plans for the weekend.

We all snapped to attention smartly. I was number one to be offered in sacrifice, being the first in the row next to the door. I stood there at military rigidity, ready with my rusty piece of junk. Capt. Davis stood just to my left, apparently inspecting my left ear. I looked straight ahead, according to strict military regulations. He continued to be mesmerized by my left ear until I finally shifted my gaze to see what the hell he saw that was so entrancing.

"Eyes straight ahead, soldier," he boomed out.

Holy shit, I thought. The captain was one of those fucking bastards who wants to play the chickenshit game.

He then stepped in front of me and nearly ripped the rifle from my hands, a grim look on his face. The grim look turned to silent shock as he viewed my rifle. He extended his right hand to Sgt. Colombresi, a gesture of supreme authority. Sgt. Colombresi, in turn, slapped a cleaning rod smartly into that outstretched mitt with a sound that shot across the room like a bullet. The rod had a gleaming white patch in its terminal eye and I saw Capt. Davis nodding approval. By then, the look on the captain's face was one of pure joy. Now for the final blow.

One quick motion and that gleaming white patch was transformed into a horrible piece of black muck.

"Two days KP, Sergeant," Capt. Davis said in a flat unemotional monotone, as my head rolled off the cutting block into the waiting basket.

Sgt. Colombresi grunted something unintelligible again, looking at me as if I deserved to be shot right where I was standing.

Capt. Davis thrust the weapon back into my hands and started to turn away.

"Captain," I said, "I'd like to explain why this weapon is in such a deplorable and lamentable condition."

I thought that if I threw a few decent words at him beyond one or two syllables, he would be more willing to listen to my explanation.

The captain stopped dead in his tracks, one leg already extended to the next man, just as if he had been stabbed in the back.

"You see, Captain, sir," I continued innocently, hoping to ignite a spark of fairness in welcoming a new man to the outfit, "I didn't bring this rifle with me from Fort McClellan when I reported this morning at nine hundred hours. This is your company's rifle assigned to me by Sgt. Brook as he sang 'Heigh-ho, heigh-ho,' telling me at the same time that it would be impossible for me to clean by inspection time."

I thought I pleaded my defense rather well.

Capt. Davis didn't even bother to turn around and look at me.

"Change that to three days KP, Sgt. Colombresi," he said and continued on with the inspection.

Thus began my long and glorious relationship with Sgt. Gaetano Colombresi. He knew he could count on me for a dirty patch on every inspection. I ended up with the distinction of being on KP more than any other man in the United States Army during World War II. In fact, I was finally awarded the Distinguished KP Service Medal, the first such in the entire country, naturally by my friend, Morelli, one that he designed himself out of a confiscated spoon, knife, and fork, in a mock ceremony on Labor Day attended by all my comrades-in-arms.

Chapter 6

Sgt. Gaetano Colombresi

Without four-letter words our military forces would find themselves speechless. As the army, navy, marines, and air force shape a
man into what they call a fighting machine, he gradually loses his
individuality and his vocabulary goes through a similar process, until
he finds himself using fewer and fewer words to express his thoughts,
and more of the words are of the four-letter variety.

I noticed this trend even as I was writing this book, transporting
myself in thought to my army days. I have put down the words just as
the men expressed themselves. There are many people who are of-
fended by such words. The words themselves, however, lose their
original meanings and become mere grunts, sounds that are vibra-
tions of air in the range of one hundred to three hundred cycles and
up to fifty or seventy-five decibels. When a tree falls in the forest, the
sound created cannot be interpreted as being offensive even though it
may sound similar, and neither should a meaningless grunt or growl.

With that, allow me to use a few meaningless grunts and growls
to describe Sgt. Gaetano Colombresi, the first sergeant of Headquarters Company, Fifth Infantry Regiment (the second oldest regiment in
the United States), 71st Infantry Division. He was a first-class
mother-fucking son-of-a-bitch of a prick.

This was the man God chose to lead us into battle, a mean little
shit who couldn't read or write (sorry, he could laboriously sign his
name with some prompting from Majchack, the company clerk), a
man who hated everybody and everything, a man who was in the

regular army fifteen years before he was promoted to private first-class, and who had an oral IQ of fifty. For some unfathomable reason, he became a favorite of Colonel Simon C. Wofford, who treated him like a pet ape.

About a month or so after my initial baptism in Headquarters Company, a notice appeared on the bulletin board (the astute reader might note the significance of the first four letters of that word "bulletin") stating that all dogtags were to be turned into the orderly room in preparation for the Inspector General's scheduled inspection of our unit.

I dutifully turned in my dogtags along with all the other men. The next day, Majchack hailed me in the company area. He looked upset.

"Sgt. Colombresi is on the warpath about your dogtags," he said. "He wants to see you immediately, if not sooner. Be prepared for a firestorm."

"Shit," I said, having learned the eloquent language of the dog-face well.

I followed him quickly down to the orderly room. There he was, the scowling, mean little shit himself, waiting to devour me.

"Zebrowsk," he grunted, not being able to pronounce any word with three syllables or more unless the word fucking was in there somewhere, "wadda fucka are you tryin' ta do ta me?"

"I don't recall doing anything to you, Sgt. Colombresi," I said, in a calm, respectful tone. I felt like adding "you fucking little runt," but thought that comment would only extend my already frequent KP duty to infinity.

"When da fuckina IG seesa yer fuckina dogtags, dats goom-bye to my fuckina ass," he said, working himself up to a frenzy.

"What is the matter with my dogtags, Sergeant?" I asked politely, looking him straight in the eye.

"Whatsa da matta, you sonamabitch, whatsa da matta? I tella you whatsa da matta. Da fuckina Catolics, dey gotta fuckina C ona dare fuckina dogtags, the fuckina Protastunts, dey gotta fuckina P ona dare fuckina dogtags, evena da fuckina Jews, dey gotta fuckina Haitch ona dare fuckina dogtags. Anda you, Zebrowsk, wadda you gotta on you fuckina dogtags? You ainta gotta shit, datsa what. You ainta gotta C, you ainta gotta P, anda you ainta gotta Haitch. Ifa you ainta C, ifa you ainta P, if you ainta Haitch, wadda da fuck are you? Now you tella me dat."

He stood there with his hands on his hips, his face twisted by his uncontrolled anger. I couldn't stand it any longer.

"I'm not a fuckina C," I said, "I'm not a fuckina P, and I'm not a fuckina Haitch. That's all there is to it, nothing more."

When I pronounced "Haitch," I really laid it on heavy, with spit flying.

I could see Majchack out of the corner of my eye. He was wagging his head back and forth and making a slitting motion with his finger across his throat.

"Hey, you maka some fuckina fun otta da way I speaka da English, huh, soldier? I'll fixa you ass on KP tilla you learna ta keepa you biga mouth shut."

And he kept his promise.

One week later, after the IG made his visit, we were notified by Majchack to pick up our dogtags.

"What's this?" I said, as Majchack handed me four sets of dogtags.

"One sheesa gotta fuckina C, one sheesa gotta fuckina P, anda one sheesa gotta fuckina Haitch, anda one sheesa gotta shit," Majchack said, in a fairly good imitation of Colombresi.

We whooped it up laughing our guts out until Colombresi stomped into the room, scowling mad as usual. When he saw me, he nearly had a fit.

"Wadda the fuck isa goin' on here?"

"I was just explaining to Zebrowsk why he has four sets of dogtags, Sergeant," Majchack said apologetically. He deliberately left off the terminal "i" in my name, but managed to get away with it.

"Never you mind explainin' any fuckina thing. Zebrowsk, get da fuck otta here."

I got out fast.

One month later, Majchack notified me that Colombresi was having me shipped off to a tank division in Kentucky.

"When?" I asked, half-expecting something like this to happen.

"Right now," he said. "Pack your duffel bag and roll up your mattress. Be ready to shove off in two hours. I told you that you were slitting your own throat."

So there I was sitting on my empty foot locker, duffel bag packed, mattress folded, looking as if the executioner was on his way, trying to convince myself that any outfit would be better without Colombresi. The barracks were empty and it was mighty lonely there. Just then, Master Sgt. Doyle happened to walk in. He was our communications platoon leader and I was under his direct jurisdiction according to the U.S. Army Table of Organization and not under Colombresi. Somebody must have notified him of my transfer even though Colombresi, I later found out, tried to keep it a secret.

"Why aren't you out with the rest of the men, Zebrowski?" he asked.

He had a pleasant Texas drawl and had always treated me decently. All the men under his command respected him.

"Colombresi is sending me to a tank outfit in Kentucky, Sergeant," I said. "I thought you knew."

Sgt. Doyle's eyes were blazing. I had never seen him that angry.

"Unpack your duffel bag, soldier, and make up your bed. You're not going anywhere. What the hell does Colombresi think he's doing shipping out one of my men?"

He was terribly upset.

"But the truck will be here in about thirty minutes, Sergeant," I said, looking at my watch.

"Don't worry about the truck, soldier. Just do as I say. If anybody goes on that truck, it'll be Colombresi himself."

He slammed the door hard as he left for the orderly room to confront Colombresi. Majchack gave us a blow-by-blow description of the battle later that day. I never did get shipped out to a tank outfit in Kentucky or anywhere else, thanks to Sergeant Doyle. I've liked people from Texas ever since.

One day after supper, Colombresi got up and after hollering out his grunt which stood for "attention," proceeded to bawl the crap out of the men who had applied for furloughs and had put distant cities such as San Francisco and Seattle as their destinations, when in reality they were only planning to go to Atlanta or some other area close to the base. Travel time was increased for distant cities. He spent at least fifteen minutes swearing at us in the vilest language his atrophied brain could muster, threatening us with a court-martial and years of hard labor. He just stopped short of a firing squad.

When he applied for a furlough himself, he listed Nome, Alaska, as his destination. Oddly enough, he had Corporal Majchack purchase railroad tickets for him to Newark, New Jersey. We all hoped that he would have listed Novosibirsk in Siberia as his destination, but we were not that lucky.

It was peaceful and quiet without Colombresi there for three weeks. I wasn't on KP or latrine duty for the entire length of time. I almost began to feel unwanted. As soon as he came back, however, he checked the latrine and the kitchen and immediately became aware that I hadn't drawn those duties in his absence.

During his furlough, for some odd reason, he developed a pathological hatred for pine needles and sand. Our company was stationed in the Sand Hill area of Fort Benning, so we had tons of both substances surrounding us. The sand and the pine needles got into our pockets, our shoes, our hair, our underwear, and even our food. Everywhere a soldier looked, he saw pine needles and sand, miles and miles. This drove Sgt. Colombresi into a frenzy. The whole thing blew up the day the mess sergeant, playing a joke on him, handed him a dish of soup full of real pine needles.

"Wadda da fuckina kinda soup isa dis?"

We were all there watching him.

"That's pine needle soup," the mess sergeant said. "It's good for you. It'll make your cock stand up straight just like a pine needle."

Colombresi swept it off the table and sent it crashing to the floor.

"Dosa fuckina pine needles, dey gotta go," he grunted. "Anda after we polica da pine needles, den we shovel out da fuckina sand."

The next day was a memorable day. I was assigned latrine duty and the rest of the men were cleaning up pine needles in the company area.

"You betta have plenty hot watta for me, Zebrowsk," Colombresi said, in one of his more affectionate tones.

I worked hard stoking up the boilers, making the latrine shine and smell like a whore house. I finally took a break and watched the men on their hands and knees in the sand picking up pine needles. Because it was an endless task, they were in no hurry. I stood there looking out the window, listening to the hot-water pipes playing a merry tune, rattling and banging against the wall.

Just then, Sgt. Colombresi came down for a shower with nothing on his skinny ass except a bath towel wrapped around his middle.

"Wadda da hella you doin', Zebrowsk, standin' dare lika dat? You gotta plenty hot wadda for me or no?"

"Yes," I said. "There's plenty of hot water for you, Sergeant. Do you hear the pipes singing 'O Sole Mio?'"

"Oh, you a funny guy, Zebrowsk," Colombresi said, not smiling. "You go out anda starta pickin' pine needles otta da sand wid da resta da bastards out dare. I'ma take a godamma shower."

I went out and joined the rest of the guys on their hands and knees. Sgt. Brawley was in charge of the pine needle brigade and was not pushing anybody.

A jeep came to a screeching halt close to the area where we were working. Brawley became rigid and let out a rasping roar that vaguely sounded like "Attention."

It was Colonel Wofford, who happened to be driving by with his driver. He was intrigued by what we were doing. He looked very unhappy.

"What are you men doing?" he asked, isolating each word in a sheath of ice. He kept tapping his thigh with his riding crop. It was rumored among the troops that he slept and showered with it.

"We are policing the area, Colonel, sir, as per general regulations," Brawley replied.

"Policing the area of what, Sergeant? It appears to me that your men are picking up pine needles out of the sand."

A little twitch appeared in Colonel Wofford's jaw.

"That's exactly what they're doing, Colonel, sir," Brawley answered.

"Is this your interpretation of what policing the area means, Sergeant?"

Colonel Wofford was building up to an eruption of volcanic proportions.

"No, sir, Colonel, sir," Brawley said.

"Then whose God-damned idea is it, Sergeant?" Colonel Wofford said, shouting as loud as he could without having a stroke.

"Sgt. Colombresi, sir," Brawley said. "After his furlough, he developed this all-consuming hatred for pine needles. He hates sand, too, sir. That's next on the list to be carted off."

Colonel Wofford appeared to be on the brink of a generalized seizure. His whole body was quivering with rage and there were a thousand twitches chasing one another in the muscles of his face.

Little by little he managed to get control of himself. Nobody moved.

"Does Sgt. Colombresi happen to be around, Sergeant?" Colonel Wofford asked politely through clenched teeth.

"He is either in the orderly room getting a lesson from Corporal Majchack on how to sign his name or he's taking a shower, sir."

Just then, Colombresi bounded out of the barracks, his towel falling off behind him, stark naked. He was facing us and didn't see Colonel Wofford.

"Wheresa dat fuckina Zebrowsk? Da barracks shesa gonna blow up. Daresa no hota wadda, justa godamma steam."

He was jumping up and down like an ape, his knuckles scraping the sand as he bent his knees.

"Sgt. Colombresi!" Colonel Wofford boomed out. His voice was like a clap of thunder rolling through the heavens.

Sgt. Colombresi stopped dead in his tracks, his head thrust forward, a shocked look on his face as he recognized the voice. He placed the toes of his right foot behind him and slowly made a perfect about face.

He snapped to sharply, saluted the colonel and stood there absolutely rigid and bare-assed.

"Sgt. Colombresi," Colonel Wofford said very slowly, pronouncing each syllable distinctly, as if he was about to spell each word, "you are out of uniform."

That was all the men needed to hear. They burst out laughing. Strict military bearing vanished.

"Cut it," Colonel Wofford thundered. "This is serious business. The next man who laughs gets a court-martial. I will not have my regiment held up to ridicule by some thoughtless individual policing pine needles. Is that understood?"

He cut the air with his riding crop and then slapped it into his left palm in complete disgust.

He turned back to Sgt. Colombresi.

"Somebody give the Sergeant something to cover up his...his...his nakedness," Colonel Wofford said, looking somewhat pleased that he had finally found an acceptable word.

Nobody moved.

"Well?" Colonel Wofford said, much louder.

Still nobody moved. Everybody remained at rigid attention, especially Colombresi, who stood there with his skinny little ass bright in the morning sun. It seemed to be exceptionally quiet except for a crow that cawed raucously somewhere in the distance.

Finally, the colonel's driver took off his necktie, knotted it around Colombresi's middle and let it hang there, a pathetic curtain.

There was not one peep anywhere, not a sound.

Colonel Wofford looked very uncomfortable, his face working. He coughed and then cleared his throat several times. His eyes were focused directly on Sgt. Colombresi's nose.

"Was this your idea, Sgt. Colombresi," he said, again very slowly, "to police the area of pine needles?"

"Yes sir, Colonel, sir," Colombresi said, proud that he was able to pronounce those simple words correctly.

"Pine needles, Sgt. Colombresi," Colonel Wofford said, almost sweetly, "are a natural part of out environment. They are not to be policed under any circumstances. And so is sand. Do I make myself clear, Sergeant?"

Slap went the riding crop into Colonel Wofford's left palm.

"Yes sir, Colonel, sir," Colombresi said. It had taken him years to memorize those four words without garbling them.

"Now have the men return all those pine needles," Colonel Wofford continued, "to their rightful place. Make sure the men rake them in to make them look natural. I believe that we can all accept pine needles and sand as part of God's plan, the same as war. Don't you think so, Sergeant Colombresi?"

"Yes sir, Colonel, sir," Colombresi answered.

"And I never want to see this kind of foolishness in my regimental area ever again. Do you understand that, Sergeant Colombresi?"

"Yes sir, Colonel, sir."

Colonel Wofford got back into his jeep, touched his riding crop to his visor as Colombresi and Brawley saluted, and drove off.

We couldn't hold back any longer. We hooted and hollered like a bunch of wild lunatics. Some of the men fell to the ground and rolled in the sand, tears in their eyes.

"Whatsa so fuckina funny?" Colombresi asked, scowling.

He stood there with his bare ass hanging out in the bright Georgia sun, a sorrowful sight. The necktie was still tied around his middle, flapping gently in the warm breeze.

"You hearda da colonel," he said, hands on his hips. "Put dosa fuckina pine needles back where shesa comin' from. And you, Zebrowsk, ifa you make so mucha steam nexa time, you ass is otta da company, no matta what Sergeant Doyla saysa."

He turned sharply, necktie flying, and walked back into the barracks, mustering what little dignity he had left.

The pipes she stopped rattling by then and the barracks she never did blow up.

Chapter 7

Night Watch

The three towns across the Danube River were burning brightly when Horsfall and Scudder took over the watch in the bell tower of the old stone church. It was 2:00 a.m. and they were both yawning and griping about having to be up. They could hear the rockets swooshing far over to the left, clusters at a time, again and again, leaving bright slashes of light across the darkness of the night.

"Why does Brawley always give us the two-o'clock watch?" Scudder said morosely.

"Because he likes us so much," Horsfall answered.

Scudder kept looking at the rockets streaking across the sky.

"There can't be much of anything left over there," he said. "I guess they won't stop until everything is burned to the ground like the air force did in Dresden with their fire bombing."

"Let them burn, the bastards," Horse growled. "I hope they get it good."

"The only problem is that a lot of innocent people get killed," Scudder said. "In Dresden, there were no military targets."

"There were no military targets in London, either," Horsfall said, "or a lot of the other cities that were bombed by the Germans. That's war, a completely stupid activity. But the German people should have thought of that when they supported a lunatic like Hitler. Now they have to suffer the consequences."

The town on this side of the river was quiet. There wasn't a sound or a movement of any kind. Most of the people had gone before we arrived.

A full moon threw a cold light over the houses creating a patch-work of black and white in the streets.

"Keep your eyes open, Scudder," Horse said. "There are a lot of places a German soldier could hide and still do plenty of damage. Some of them are stupid enough to fight to the last man. For what, the Fuhrer?"

He laughed derisively.

The two of them squatted next to the field telephone that Densman and his wire crew had strung for them, as if waiting to hear it ring at any moment. Their faces were tired and drawn in the narrow shaft of pale light entering through a small triangular window in front of them. The rockets continued for another fifteen minutes and then suddenly ceased firing. Only the crackling flames, mirrored in the muddy water of the river, could be heard.

Horse made a sniffing sound.

"What the hell stinks in here?" he asked, making a face.

He got up, feeling the stiffness in his knees from squatting too long. He stretched, yawned loudly, and started poking around in the dark corners of the small room.

"I don't know," Scudder said. "Sit down, will you? You're making too damned much noise, Horse. If there are any Germans around, they'll certainly hear us. We're not supposed to give our position away, you know."

Horse ignored him. He continued to check the room. He finally stumbled over something on the floor and swore.

"Well, what do you know, a dead German soldier," he said. "They must have been using this tower as a lookout just like we are."

He went to the window and opened it.

"What the hell are you doing, Horse?"

"I think we can just about squeeze him through this window and we'll be rid of the stink," Horse answered.

"That will really wake up the whole damn town, Horse. Why don't you just leave him alone? He'll never fit through that window, anyway."

"I don't give a diddly fuck about the noise," Horse said. "He'll fit through the window all right. Did you ever notice how much smaller people seem to be when they're dead?"

They stuffed the dead German through the narrow triangular opening and heard the body fall to a roof fifty feet below with a loud thud. It then rolled a few feet and finally landed on the pavement. Scudder stuck his head out the window and vomited.

"You know, Scudder," Horse said, disgusted, "sometimes you're just a big pain in the ass."

"I couldn't help it," Scudder said. "The smell and the sound of him landing on the ground made me sick."

Horse lit a cigarette and slouched against the wall. He half-closed his eyes and listened to his own steady breathing. He felt he could go to sleep very easily. Scudder would wake him if anything was happening. He knew he could count on that.

He took one last look at Scudder. He still had his head out the window, breathing in the fresh air and watching the street for any movement down below.

It was quiet now that the rockets had stopped.

A board creaked on the stairs and both men jerked up quickly. Scudder banged his head against the window frame and winced.

"Godammit, keep quiet," Horse whispered gruffly.

"Horse...," Scudder started to say.

"Shut up."

They waited in the dark, hardly daring to breathe. The sound drifted up to them again, undoubtedly a footstep. Someone was climbing the stairs slowly and trying to be very quiet.

"It's too early for our relief," Scudder whispered.

"Keep quiet, godammit," Horse said.

They sat there listening to the stairs creaking as the person slowly ascended. They didn't move a muscle. The sound came again, barely audible, but definite.

Horse pulled out his Luger from the holster below his left armpit and gently slipped the safety off.

"I'll go with you, Horse," Scudder said softly.

"No. You stay by the phone."

Horse slipped out of the room and crept down the stairs slowly and carefully in the dark, holding the Luger tightly in his right hand. He waited on the landing below until he heard the sound again. Someone was definitely climbing the stairs one step at a time, waiting a full minute or two between each move.

He could feel the sweat pour out of his skin and a sudden spasm racked his body. He settled back in the darkness and waited, holding his breath, his heart pumping rapidly, a burning dryness in his throat.

A shadowy figure appeared on the top step and moved forward, close against the wall. The floor creaked slightly. As Horse leaped forward from a crouch, swinging the gun in a wide arc, he tripped over a loose board in the floor and went sprawling against the approaching figure. The gun slipped out of his hand and slid away in the dark as he crashed to the floor. The two grappled for an instant before Horse suddenly stopped.

"What the hell?" he cried out. "Was machs du?"

"Bitteshön...," a frightened voice replied.

"Well, Jesus Christ," Horse said. "A German dame!"

He got up and felt his muscles relax, his body filling his sweat-dampened clothes. He expelled a long, noisy breath in relief.

"Come here, you," he said roughly, grabbing the woman by the wrists. He pulled her down the stairs to a window through which the moon cast a feeble light. The woman's face was thin and drawn. The lines around her eyes and mouth made her youthful features appear older.

She coughed and put a handkerchief to her mouth.

"Are you sick?" Horse asked.

"No," she said. "I just feel very weak. I've had nothing to eat for the last several days. I've been too frightened to go out. I didn't know anyone was here until I heard a loud thump on the roof and some voices."

Her English was perfect.

She started to cry, her whole body shaking in a violent spasm. She fell to her knees, coughing hard.

Horse pulled away and stood looking down at her until she finally stopped coughing. Her body continued to shudder periodically.

"What's the matter with you?" he said.

"Nothing," she said. "Nothing. I told you I just feel weak from not eating."

"OK," he said. "Stay here and I'll get something for you to

eat."

He ran up the stairs to the room where Scudder was huddled in the corner, his rifle aimed directly at the doorway.

"Anything going on up here?" Horse asked.

"No," Scudder said. "What the hell was all that noise? Did you fall on the stairs? I thought the Germans were coming in for sure."

"No, that was just a German dame, that's all," Horse said. "With a little luck, I just might be able to exchange some K rations for some action in the sack."

"You're going to cause a lot of trouble, Horse," Scudder said, grabbing him by the shoulder. "What if something happens up here and I need you right away? I think you should just leave her alone. If Brawley ever finds out you left your post, it'll be your ass."

"Brawley's not going to find out, is he, Scudder, because you're not going to tell him. And as for leaving her alone, don't be crazy."

Horse shrugged Scudder off.

"I'll be back in about thirty minutes," he said. "And don't worry, godammit. Nothing's going to happen up here. Everything's quiet now and I'm pretty sure it's going to stay that way. In an hour, we'll be off watch and back in our fart sacks."

He picked up a couple of K rations lying on the floor next to the telephone. He left Scudder standing in the dark and went down the stairs two at a time. He had forgotten all about his Luger that he had dropped on the landing.

He led the girl to a small room off the altar. He lit one of the candles there and stood looking at her. She was disheveled and her clothes were dirty. The flame of the candle was reflected in her tearing eyes and she looked pitiful.

"Couldn't we go somewhere else?" she asked, scared. "I don't want to stay here."

"No," Horse said. "I'm on watch and I have to stay here in case anything happens."

He looked around the room.

"This room is fine," he said. "What's the matter with it?"

"There's a dead German soldier in the next room," she said, starting to cry again.

"If he's dead, he won't bother us," Horse said.

"I killed him," she sobbed, her voice weak and fading. She swayed on her feet and put a hand to her face. She was trembling.

"I didn't want to kill him," she said, still crying. "He was a thoughtless brute and slapped me around all the time. He deserted from the Wehrmacht and was hiding here from his unit. He said he didn't want to die fighting a useless war, but he died anyway."

She slid to the floor and sobbed heavily, her face in her hands.

"Did you shoot him with his own gun?" Horse asked.

"No. I killed him yesterday with a pair of scissors, just before you Americans came into our town. He was asleep, but he awoke just before I did it. He began to hit me again and I stuck the scissors into his neck. He seemed so surprised, as if he didn't think that I would ever do anything like that. It was awful. I didn't want to do it, but he forced me. Now I'm truly sorry he's dead."

She was sprawled at his feet, her head against the floor, crying loudly now. Another spasm of coughing shook her slender body and her shoulders jerked convulsively. Her breath kept catching in her throat.

"And the other dead man upstairs in the bell tower?" Horse said. "What happened to him?"

"Erich killed him. They were drinking all night and started to fight. Erich shot him."

Horse took the candle and went to the door of the adjacent room and looked in. A narrow bed was in the corner. The German soldier lay under a pile of rumpled-up bed covers with a pair of scissors sticking out from the base of his neck. His eyes were wide open and he still had a surprised look on his face, as if he couldn't quite believe what had happened. He was dead all right. Horse wrapped the covers around the body and dragged it out of the room and out the front door of the church. The German was a big son-of-a-bitch and Horse was breathing hard by the time he had finished dumping him.

The girl was still sobbing on the floor when he came back. He opened the two K rations and spread the crackers and the tins of meat on the one table in the room. He went over to the girl and pulled her to her feet. She leaned against him, almost falling.

"You don't have to cry anymore," he said. "Nobody's going to hurt you and you don't have to be afraid."

71

He led her to the table.

"Eat," he said, pointing to the food. "It's just army food and rather tasteless, but it will fill your belly."

She looked at him incredulously.

"We were told that the Americans would first rape us and then kill us," she said, not moving.

"Well, that's a half-truth if I ever heard one," Horse said, laughing roughly. "I don't want a damn thing from you. Just eat."

He went to the door and took the key out of the lock.

"I'll lock the door so the other soldiers won't bother you," he said. "Don't make any noise or the whole army will be here."

He looked at his watch.

"I'll be back in a little while, as soon as my duty is over. Then we can talk. Don't be afraid."

The girl stood in the middle of the room leaning against the table, still not moving toward the food.

"Eat," he said again. "For Christ sakes, eat. Do you want me to spoon feed you like a baby?"

He slipped out of the room and locked the door.

At first, Scudder didn't say anything when Horse came back up the stairs, huffing and puffing from the steep climb. They just sat there silently, not even looking at one another.

"Well?" Scudder finally said.

"What do you mean, 'well'?" Horse said.

"What did you do with the German dame?"

"She's downstairs eating," Horse said.

"And...?" Scudder said.

"Why all the questions? I didn't know you'd be that interested. She'll still be there when we finish our watch."

"Then what?" Scudder kept on.

"Then we'll see what happens," Horse said. "I'll play it by ear. If you want a chance at her, I'm sure that can be arranged."

"Stop screwing around. Just leave her alone. Don't be a stupid ass."

"I'm not asking for your advice, you know, Scudder," Horse said. "And I know what I'm doing, so get off my back."

Scudder shook his head.

"Go ahead, then. Go fuck your head off. I don't give a damn."

Scudder went to the window and watched the fires burning across the river. They weren't as bright as they had been before, but they looked like they were going to be burning a long time.

"That's exactly what I plan to do," Horse said. "And I expect you to keep your trap shut. Do you understand?"

"Yes, I believe I do."

"And tomorrow, if you get a bullet crashing through your fuckin' skull or if an 88 spills your stinking guts into a ditch and you begin to smell like that rotten German soldier we threw out the window, then maybe you'll understand even more. But by then, it'll be too late."

Horse waved his hand in disgust.

"Aah, what's the use in talking?" he said.

"You do what you think you have to do, Horse," Scudder said, "and I'll do what I have to do. Don't worry about me. Just leave me out of your plans."

"Don't worry about that," Horse said derisively. "We're on different wave lengths."

Twenty minutes later their relief came up.

"If you guys talked any louder, the Germans wouldn't have any trouble finding you even if they were blind," one of the men said. "Anything exciting going on?"

"Not a thing," Horse said. "Just don't fall asleep or you might wake up with your throat slit."

Outside the church, Horse put his hand on Scudder's shoulder.

"Remember," he said. "I'm counting on you to keep your mouth shut."

Scudder shrugged him off and didn't say a word. Horse went back into the dark church and quietly unlocked the door. The girl was sitting on the floor, her back to the wall. She had eaten only a small portion of the food. Horse saw that the candle was nearly burned out. He blew it out and stumbled in the dark to where the girl was sitting quietly.

He started fumbling with the front of her dress with his right hand, sliding his left hand up her thigh. He was tired and he wasn't going to waste any time.

"No," the girl said. "No."

She started to cry again.

"Please don't," she sobbed. "Please."

"I'm not going to hurt you," Horse said. "But if you want me to be nice to you, then you'll have to be nice to me. You understand that, don't you?"

"Then you are going to kill me after all," she said. "Just like they warned us you would."

"Don't be foolish," Horse said. "Nobody's going to kill you."

He gradually forced her to the floor, rolling on top of her, all the while his hands were pulling up her dress and exploring.

He tried to kiss her but she moved her head to one side.

"Don't be stupid and make me mad," he said, pinning both her arms down. His sheer weight made it difficult for her to move.

"That's what I like," he said. "Just a little resistance to make it more interesting."

He stuck his tongue into her mouth while she was gasping for air and she bit down on it.

"You little bitch," he yelled out in pain.

He slapped her hard across the mouth. It was easy after that. She offered no further resistance. She lay there without moving, crying softly. Horse was grunting in rhythmic tones as he thrust back and forth.

"Now wasn't that easy?" Horse asked sweetly. "No sense in fighting. Otherwise, you could have gotten hurt and I didn't want to do that."

He rolled over and felt completely exhausted. The girl was on her side, knees drawn up, sobbing softly in the dark.

After awhile, Horse fell asleep. He snored loudly.

He heard the loud crack of the Luger at the same time that the bullet smashed into the wall next to his head. He was suddenly wide awake, his nostrils burning with the smell of the gunfire. He rolled quickly on the floor as the second slug barely pierced his side like a streak of lightning. He got up and ran to the door, the pistol exploding again and again with the bullets slapping into the pews, splintering the wood. He could hear her running and crying behind him. He scooted out the front door of the church like a man on fire, feeling the cold night air against his hot sweating face. He hit the ground rolling to his right. He lay there for a moment, breathing hard, his heart pumping wildly. After a few moments, he heard her crying just a few feet from him and pure panic overwhelmed his brain. He reached for the Luger under his left armpit. The holster was empty and he remembered he had lost the pistol in the dark on the stairs in the church. He turned slowly to face her.

She stood in the doorway of the church, a frail figure in the dark, barely discernible in the shadows. Still sobbing and trembling, she took careful aim at Horse for one last shot.

Scudder, hearing the shots, came running back, holding his rifle tightly in both hands. He saw Horse lying on the ground, looking at the girl holding the Luger pointed at him. Scudder lifted his M1 and taking careful aim, shot her in the head. She sprawled down the steps without uttering a sound.

There were no bullets left in the pistol that she still clutched with both hands.

Chapter 8

Reconnaissance

We had been going through a dark and dense forest of pines when we shot out into the bright, early morning sunlight, skirting a rapidly plunging river, our eyes blinking, the dust swirling and gritty in our mouths. The German soldiers were there in front of us, scattered about the hillside like a bunch of sheep peacefully grazing.

"Jerries," Horse yelled loudly as his jeep came to a screeching stop. Squinting against the sun, Horse swung the heavy .30 caliber machine gun around and grunted as he pulled the trigger, his lips pulled tight against his teeth. He got off three or four quick bursts before Tulley got to him and knocked him aside.

"You stupid son-of-a-bitch," Tulley roared. "Can't you see they're unarmed?"

Horse came up with his mouth wide open, snarling like a grizzly bear.

"What the fuck do you think you're doing, you bastard?" he roared back.

He lifted his right arm like a club and before Tulley could get out of the way, struck him across the chin. Tulley went down like a sack of grain, his helmet scraping a rock as he fell off the jeep. Horse jumped down after him and swung his boot to kick him in the ribs. He was breathing hard. Tulley saw the boot coming and rolled quickly to avoid the kick. He felt a sharp pain in his right shoulder as the boot made contact. Morelli grabbed Horse from behind and the other men crowded around. Sgt. Brawley rushed in, pushing everybody aside.

"Take it easy, Horse," he said. "Do you want to kill him? We're supposed to be fighting the Germans, not each other."

Horse shrugged Morelli off and stood there breathing through his mouth, his face twisted in a violent fit of anger. Tulley got up slowly, rubbing his jaw. He could feel the pain shooting up from his mouth into his left ear. He spit some blood into the dry dust of the road. He was bleeding slightly from a split in his lower lip and felt it beginning to swell. He didn't bother to look at Horse.

Sgt. Brawley turned and watched the Germans on the hill.

"Christ," he said. "What a fucking mess this is."

There were at least three dead soldiers and about another half dozen or so moaning and writhing on the ground. Twelve more were standing up with their hands on their heads in a state of shock, their faces drawn with fear. After the loud clattering of the machine gun, it seemed terribly quiet.

Tulley went down to the stream. It was moving quickly over the rocks, making a loud rushing noise. He bent over and splashed the ice-cold water over his mouth and jaw.

"We can't do anything with these poor bastards," Sgt. Brawley said. "We'll notify the 1st Battalion and they'll clean up here and take care of the wounded. Let's move out."

We climbed back into the jeeps and drove off, leaving the Germans staring at us in complete bewilderment. Tulley looked at them for a while and then turned away, squinting against the sun at the jeeps up ahead. Horse was standing up in the back of his jeep, bracing himself against the heavy .30 caliber.

"No sense getting mad over some wounded Germans, Tulley," Morelli said, looking back at him over his right shoulder. He was driving slowly and drifting farther behind to avoid the dust kicked up by the other jeeps.

"That son-of-a-bitch Horse will do the same thing again if he gets another chance, you know," Tulley said. "He's trigger-happy and thinks he's some kind of avenging angel. He doesn't realize that most of those poor bastards would rather be out fishing or hunting instead of dying out here."

"Yeah," Sgt. Brawley said, "but not all of them. Most of them have been indoctrinated and want to fight for the Fatherland and deserve what they're getting. Just remember how they slaughtered the I and R Platoon of the 66th Regiment in Regensburg."

"Sure and I agree with you," Tulley answered. "Many of them did a lot of rotten things, especially the SS troops, but it's hard to justify shooting unarmed soldiers. In fact, it's illegal."

"The whole fucking war is illegal," Morelli said. "But I think Horse pulled the trigger instinctively, you know. We came out of the woods so fast where it was dark and into the bright sunlight so quickly that we were on top of them before we knew what was happening. Horse started shooting immediately. Anyway, it would be better to forget the whole damn thing. We can't undo what's been done."

"Horse is a damn butcher," Tulley said.

Nobody spoke after that. Tulley spit into the dust again. He was still bleeding slightly from his lower lip, tasting the salty blood in his mouth. He looked at the river splashing along the road. It spilled out quickly over the smooth rocks in its bed, catching the sun that was edging up slowly in the sky and blinding him with the reflection. He sat there quietly, eyes half-closed against the dust, letting his body bounce with the motion of the jeep while he listened to the steady sound of the motor.

The sun was high when Sgt. Brawley gave the order to pull in among some trees that lined the river where it turned sharply around a hill. The men piled out and leaned over the water, ducking their heads, coming up with red faces stinging, blowing water out of their mouths in a fine spray, laughing and hollering. Tulley sat on the bank of the river and pulled off his boots and socks. The water was cold, making him suck in his breath. The river was clean and quick under a clear, blue sky. He and Morelli walked in the water along the bank, slipping over the smooth rocks that bruised their feet, but felt good. They stretched out on the grass, feeling the heat of the sun, their legs still stinging from the cold, mountain stream.

Sgt. Brawley came by and tossed each of them a K ration.

"No chicken or eggs today," he said sadly.

Horse walked up laughing, shaking water out of his hair into everybody's face. He sat down against a tree, rubbing his back against the bark. He stuck a cigarette in his mouth but didn't light it.

He played with it, moving it back and forth with his lips.

Sgt. Brawley looked at him for a few minutes without saying a word and then decided to sit close by.

Tulley could see Horse watching him as he opened a can of cheese from the K ration.

"I never shot so damn many Germans before in my life, Sam," Horse said laughing. "Somebody should give me a medal. I had enough adrenaline pumping through me to keep an entire army going. The smell of blood makes you feel good."

Sgt. Brawley looked at Horse.

"You don't get medals for shooting unarmed soldiers," he said.

Tulley saw Morelli shaking his head in disgust.

"Well, they should," Horse kept on. "Then we wouldn't have to feed those bastards. The Germans have been running their asses off now for three solid months and they still don't know enough to quit."

He continued to play with the cigarette between his teeth. Tulley knew he was looking in his direction. He just watched the river. He had had enough of Horse.

But Horse kept right on talking.

"If they want to fight to the last man, that's OK with me. All I want is to have the very last German all to myself."

Horse laughed, staring intently at Tulley. Sgt. Brawley and Morelli watched both of them closely.

"I know what I'd do to the last German son-of-a-bitch," Horse said. "I'd tear the fucker apart, bit by bit. I'd pull his fingernails off. 'That's for the 66th I and R,' I'd say to him. I'd poke his eyes out with a bayonet. 'That's for the 66th, too.' I'd build a fire and stick his feet into the burning wood. 'That's for the 66th, too, you motherfucker.' Then I'd cut off his cock and watch him screaming in pain as he bled to death and I'd think of all those American boys who had to die because of him."

Tulley kept his head down, looking at the marks his teeth made in the cheese he was eating. He heard the river splashing over the rocks.

Horse kept going.

"He'd beg me to finish him nice and quick, but I'd take my time. It would be a great pleasure to see him suffer, so why would I hurry?

How about you, Tulley? What would you do if you had the last German soldier all to yourself?"

He was smiling, enjoying every minute of his monologue.

Tulley got up without looking at Horse. He saw Brawley motioning to him, hooking his thumb toward the river and wagging his head back and forth, warning him to stay away from Horse and not to answer him.

Horse jumped up and followed Tulley. He wasn't going to let up that easily.

"Come on, Tulley," he said. "Tell us what you'd do if you had the last German soldier all to yourself."

Tulley heard Horse walking close behind him, breathing hard like a bull preparing to attack after his pasture had been invaded. Tulley turned around to face him. They were at the edge of the stream and Tulley couldn't go any farther. He was ready to make his stand. He knew Horse was not just playing a game. He meant to start a fight with Tulley and nobody was going to stop him.

"Lay off, Horse," Sgt. Brawley said, coming up quickly from behind. "You had your fun. Now get off his back."

"Hell, Sam," Horse said smiling. "I was just asking Tulley a simple question, that's all. I don't know why you're getting so upset."

He threw his hands up in complete innocence.

"I'll tell you what I'd do, you fucking bastard," Tulley said, each word clear and distinct, like bullets exploding out of his mouth. He held his hands in front of him, waiting for Horsfall's lunge. Horse was built like an ox and had a good hundred pounds on Tulley.

"Shut up, Tulley," Sgt. Brawley said. "That's enough of this childish bullshit. Let's mount up and move out."

"I'd give him a gun," Tulley said, ignoring Brawley's remark, "and point you out and say, 'Shoot the bastard for everybody's sake.'"

Tulley saw Horsfall's hands shoot out like grappling hooks, grabbing him by the throat before he could make a move. He tried to bring up his right knee to jam him in the crotch, but Horse was in too close.

"God damn your fucking hide," Horse growled.

Tulley saw Brawley and Morelli grab Horse by the shoulders and try to pull him off. Tulley felt the strength go out of his legs as he tried to breathe. He fell to the ground and Horse fell on top of him, a two-hundred-and-fifty-pound slab of meat, knocking the rest of the air out of his lungs. Tulley pushed hard as everything started to turn black and both of them rolled off the bank into the river. Tulley ended up on top of Horse, who was kicking and hitting the air with both fists and sucking in water. The cold water revived Tulley. Everything stopped spinning. He sat there on top of Horse, not minding the cold water at all, watching Horse turn blue with his face under water.

Morelli pulled Tulley onto the bank while Sam Brawley sat Horse up in the water. Horse was dazed, coughing, snorting, spitting, and swearing.

"Where's that son-of-a-bitch?" he growled.

"Once more, Horse," Sgt. Brawley said, "and your ass is out of this platoon."

Horse was laughing as water dripped down his face. His hair was plastered against his skull.

"What's a little fun, Sam?" he asked.

Tulley stood up, his legs rubbery, while Morelli supported him against a tree. He turned away from Morelli and puked his head off. His stomach was in a knot and his hands were shaking.

The rest of the men were standing lined up along the bank of the river, looking at Horse who was still sitting in the water and laughing.

"Horse, what the hell are you doing sitting in the river like a big, water-soaked buffalo?" one of them said.

"Just showing Tulley what I'd do to the last German soldier in Alley-mand if I had him all to myself," Horse said. He scratched his head.

"You know, come to think of it," he continued, "there ain't much difference between Tulley and the Germans."

"God damn you, Horsfall," Sgt. Brawley said. "Didn't you hear me straight? I told you to keep your big mouth shut."

Horse stopped laughing. He stood up, water dripping from his clothes. The men stared at him, not knowing what to do or say.

The two men took off their clothes, wrung them out, and put them back on. Tulley was shivering.

Sgt. Brawley gave the order to move out and the men went back to their jeeps. Fortunately, the sun was still hot. Within a short time, though, as we pulled away from the river on a road that led to higher ground, ugly black clouds began to smear the sky. A light wind began to blow. It made Tulley tremble spasmodically in his wet clothes. His whole body ached and felt stiff. The dust from the road was lifted by the jeeps even higher in huge clouds as we began to go faster. It seemed to float forever in the air before settling back down to the ground.

Morelli kept looking at the sky as it continued to darken.

"It's going to rain," he said. "It'll be good to get rid of some of this dust."

Tulley sat with his right hand over his nose, still breathing hard. He blinked his eyes and felt the dust grit in the corners of his eyelids, just like the sand in the clip release of his M1. His chest ached from all the water he had swallowed and pain throbbed in his jaw. His throat felt raw and his lip had started to bleed again.

"I was a damn fool," Tulley finally said, tasting the dust in his mouth.

"Anybody's a fool who fights Horse with anything less than a gun in his hand," Morelli said.

The country became hilly and Tulley watched the trees lining the road for any sign of the Germans as the jeeps slowed down going around blind turns and up over the crests of the hills. The ground was still bare and brown in many spots but the spring rains had patched the countryside with green, and now the dust was settling on the trees and the grass and the shrubs in a thick layer, leaving the roads edged with gray, bleak and dry in the fading afternoon light.

More and more German equipment lay abandoned along the road, 88s, mortars, panzerfausts, ammunition, and empty ammo cases. The Germans were retreating in a mighty big hurry. Tulley kept watching the side of the road for any sign of life, holding his rifle on the ready, thinking how the American armored divisions had ripped through the countryside, leaving large German units relatively intact waiting for the infantry to move up. Some of those units were very willing to surrender, but others were determined to fight to the end. That's what made life interesting, dangerous, and very uncertain.

Tulley looked up at the sky as a few raindrops hit him in the face. The clouds had become blacker, blotting out the sun entirely and the trees began to bend with the wind, their new leaves rustling.

The lead jeep stopped quickly and Corporal Stulek waved his hand in the air and pointed to the trees along the road. Sgt. Brawley traced a circle in the air and we all piled out of the jeeps and scattered. Apparently, Stulek had seen or heard something that made him stop so suddenly. Up ahead, just beyond a slight bend in the road, Tulley saw an old farmhouse. Beyond that, the ground rose sharply. A stone wall to the right of the house followed the hill to its crest and then cut across in front of some pines and came down on the other side. There were scattered rocks in the fields and in front of the house, a small pond. Everything was quiet. We knelt behind the trees and watched the house. Two 88's, aimed at the bend in the road, stood in front of it with cases of shells scattered about.

Tulley could see one side of the wall that ran up the hill. Sgt. Brawley was about ten yards from him, pointing to the house and then at Horse, who was lying behind a huge boulder about another ten yards from Brawley. Horse got up and ran across the road, dropping into the ditch near the wall. Just as he slid up to the edge of the wall, looking carefully into the yard, a door slammed in the rear of the house. A young boy in civilian clothes started running up the hill. He was fast. Horse disappeared over the wall and Tulley kept watching the boy. He was near the top of the hill where the wall jutted across its summit when the single shot rang out. The boy's body jerked, but he kept going until he reached the wall, awkwardly now, grabbing for the stones, staggering, slipping to his knees, on all fours finally, but still moving, crawling in a slow agonizing motion and then falling and lying still. Tulley dug his fingers into the hard dirt until he couldn't stand the pain. He lay flat with his mouth wide open against the pine needles that covered the ground. A muscle began to twitch in the back of his neck where his helmet pressed coldly. He closed his eyes and breathed heavily. The shot still rang in his ears and he kept seeing the young boy dropping near the wall. He was running, his body jerking, his hands grabbing for the wall, his fingers slipping, falling to his knees, then crawling in that slow, agonizing motion, his face contorted with pain, blood oozing from his lips. Tulley kept his eyes shut tight until they ached and colors merged and gradually blotted out the boy running, jerking, and dropping, but the shot continued to ring out in his ears.

Tulley opened his eyes and saw Morelli looking at him. Tulley didn't say anything. He started to crawl over to the tree where Sgt. Brawley knelt hunched over waiting for Horse to return.

The house was quiet. Tulley looked across the road and saw Horse crawling over the wall and back into the ditch, his face dirty. He was smiling. Brawley waved at him to come back.

"What the hell did you kill him for, Horse?" Brawley asked. "He was just a kid and I didn't see a gun on him."

"You saw him running, didn't you?" Horse said. "What the hell did you want me to do? How do you know if the Germans that belong to those big guns ain't on the other side of that hill?"

Horse looked over at Tulley and then quickly up the hill.

"Damn!" he said.

Tulley saw the kid pulling himself over the wall. Horse raised his rifle quickly, but Tulley shoved the barrel aside as he squeezed his shot off and the bullet slammed into a tree. Horse dropped his rifle and jumped up to grab Tulley, but Brawley quickly got between them.

"I ought to kill you, Tulley," Horse said.

"Take it easy, Horse," Brawley said. "You kill enough as it is. You don't have to kill kids."

"Christ," Horse said. "You sound like Tulley. What the hell do you think we're over here for, a dance?"

It really began to rain then, long sheets of water that slapped against the ground and whipped through the trees. It was getting dark.

"Well, are you going to let me get him or aren't you?" Horse said. "A thousand German soldiers could be on the other side of that hill. In another five minutes, we won't be worth a crap."

"Let me go, Sam," Tulley said.

"You!" Horse said. "Christ, don't make me laugh."

"You go ahead, Tulley," Sgt. Brawley said. "Be careful of that kid. He may be armed."

Brawley put his hand on Tulley's shoulder.

"I'll give you fifteen minutes to get up there and scout around," he said. "See if the kid is dead. If we don't hear from you by then, I'll send up Horse."

Horse grunted.

"I'll see you in fifteen minutes, Tulley," he said sneeringly.

Tulley slipped through the trees and came out on the edge of the road. The rain came down hard, beating against the ground and filling the ditches quickly. The water rushed along the road, eating into its sides until it was muddy with clay and twigs. Leaves swirled on its surface. The force of the rain made a roaring sound in the woods.

He ran to the edge of the wall on the side away from the house and started up the hill. He kept his head below the top of the wall. He took one last look backward. He saw Morelli clasping both hands, silently wishing him good luck. The rain spattered on his back and felt cold on his neck. He was trembling violently.

When he came to the point where the wall turned abruptly and ran along the top of the hill, he hugged the ground more closely. The rocks of the wall were slick with rain that dripped through the cracks. In places there were lichens that stood out sharp and green against the dull mottled gray of the rocks. They smelled sweet and clean with the rain.

He looked back once again and saw the dirt road below with the trees on the other side where the platoon was waiting for him and where Horse was laughing to himself. The clouds appeared blacker from where he lay and the rain seemed to pour down harder. He held his rifle under his right arm and looked carefully around the corner of the wall. He could see the boy about forty yards from him. He crawled to him slowly. The boy's eyes were wide open, his pupils dilated. His face appeared peaceful in death. His hands were clutching his chest where blood had soaked his clothes. He was about fourteen and he was dead and Horse had killed him. Tulley leaned his rifle against the wall and lifted the boy's head onto his knee, watching the rain beat against his face that looked so young. Blood had trickled out of the corners of his mouth and the rain was washing it away.

Tulley laid the boy down. He felt very tired and his jaw began to ache again from clenching his teeth so tightly. He closed his eyes for a moment and saw the thin figure running, then jerking as the shot rang out and finally dropping near the wall. He opened them again quickly to blot out that image. He looked up at the sky where the black clouds swirled and poured down a heavy rain. It was cold against his face and he knew it wasn't going to let up.

He picked up his rifle and started back along the wall. Just as he turned the corner, he looked back at the boy. He was a small, huddled mass against the wall. In another few minutes, if he didn't start down, he thought to himself, his old friend Horse would be starting up the hill, smiling, and the two of them would be there all alone. That would be good, he said to himself, that would be very good. He moved from the edge of the wall and settled down behind a large boulder in a depression about ten yards away. That was as good a place as any to wait for Horse.

He sat there listening to the rain rush through the trees and pound the earth. Then another sound, a soft crying, made him listen more intently. He looked back to the boy and saw an old man in civilian clothes with a rifle, holding the boy's head and caressing and kissing his face. He was sobbing softly.

At that moment, Tulley heard a sound coming from the other direction, from the road, a twig snapping and he knew that Horse was on his way.

The old man must have heard the sound, too. Tulley saw him lay the boy's head down and then stretch out on the wet ground, aiming the rifle directly at the spot where the wall made a right angle turn, the exact spot where Horse would be in another two minutes. Tulley started down the hill silently. He knew he didn't have to wait for Horse anymore.

Chapter 9

Crossing the Danube

"**W**hat the fuck are we doing here, Morelli?" I asked my good buddy.

"What the fuck does it matter?" Morelli answered. "We're here and we're going to do exactly what we're told to do, just like robots, even if the orders are issued by some idiot nicely sequestered in some safe haven far away from here. Thinking about it is only going to make us all feel rotten. I'm going to clean my Luger. That way, my mind will be occupied with something sweet and simple and I won't be tempted to go AWOL and forget about this whole God-damned mess."

We were sitting in an old cement house on the edge of the "beautiful", blue Danube, a swift muddy, brown river that sliced through the city of Regensburg. We heard the artillery shells slipping through the air above us in both directions. Every so often we'd hit the floor when one sounded like a short one. The poor bastards of the line companies were in the process of crossing the river in boats, outboard motors roaring, the propellers churning the muddy water. The Germans were well entrenched on the hills across the swollen river, covering the area with machine gun fire. They were knocking off our infantry without any difficulty as our troops attempted to push across and establish a foothold on the other side.

Our platoon had a grandstand view of the entire maneuver and it was plain to see that our infantrymen had started their crossing before the Germans had been knocked out of their positions on the bluff.

Our artillery was not effective because the shells were falling far behind the German lines. While we watched, the Germans let loose with a devastating mortar barrage that decimated our troops, forcing them to pull back. There were many bodies floating down the river with the swift current. After this brief retreat, our troops concentrated their mortar and artillery fire on the bluff overlooking the river.

In the meantime, we started to clean our pistols and rifles, knowing that we were going to follow the infantry in a few hours.

"All our lives we've been taught that life is sacred and precious," I said to the men sitting at the table busily cleaning their equipment. "Some holy son-of-a-bitch even went so far as to say there are no atheists in foxholes, trying to suggest that fear is the reason why God is at your side in times of danger. That is pure, unadulterated bullshit. The truth of the matter is, you'll never find God by your side in a foxhole. You're all alone out there and your fear causes you to regress and beg God to join you, just like you did when you were a child frightened in the dark, calling for your mother and father. And does God join you in that hole our politicians forced you to enter? Hell no! He's too goddamn smart to do something that stupid. He falls back on that old doctrine of 'free will'. 'Hey buddy,' He says, 'you got yourself in this mess, now you can get yourself out.' What a friend to have in desperate times. Just a snap of His fingers, if He has fingers, and you'd be safe as a baby in the womb, suspended in your mother's front-yard swimming pool. But no, He has forsaken you in that stinking hole as you wait for your crap-filled guts to be torn open by an artillery shell, just as He has forsaken our infantrymen in those boats and us here in this house."

"Zeb's at it again," Morelli said. "We're in for our weekly dose of philosophy. And today, he seems to be in exceptional form."

"So here we are," I continued, "after four months of basic infantry training, eight weeks in my case, that consisted mostly, for me anyway, of cleaning a variety of shithouses and the sump drains in mess hall kitchens, with the final realization that our lives aren't worth a fuck; fighting to make the world safe for a bunch of undeserving bastards back home. Why? I'll tell you why: because the politicians failed in doing their job. So in the end, who pays the price? Old GI Joe, of course. We're the ones who get sacrificed.

Wouldn't it be easier to kill all the politicians instead and start all over again?"

Someone farted and I continued.

"At this very moment, some son-of-a-bitch with one or two stars on his collar is calculating how many of us will die here and how many will die there, concluding no matter how many, that that's not so bad. 'Hmmm,' he says to himself, 'only one hundred and fifty dead here and one hundred dead there.' Then he reaches for his Scotch and water and takes a long satisfying swig. He smacks his lips and pushes back on his chair, crosses his legs, takes a deep drag on his foot-long Churchillian cigar, and then lets out smoke in a long, luxurious exhalation. He looks out the window and sees the rain, the snow, and the mud, but only for an instant, because he knows it might bother him thinking of those poor dogfaces out on the front lines, and that might interfere with his strategic planning. He stands up, stretches, and farts, wondering if the loss of life will be significant enough to earn him a Distinguished Service Medal. He reaches for his combat jacket that is already adorned with so many medals that there is very little room left, because the awarding of medals is directly related to the distance you are from the front, meaning the farther you are, the more medals you receive. He then goes outside where a beautiful Wac is waiting to drive him to his destination. He says to her, 'Tonight at eleven?' and she answers, 'Yes, sir.' And off they go into the twilight, both smiling and saying simultaneously, 'Isn't war hell?'"

"I'm ready to kill that son-of-a-bitch and his whore right now," Morelli yelled out. "Where the fuck is he?"

"After listening to your harangue, Zebrowski," Sgt. Brawley said, "I think we should all go out and get piss-assed drunk and forget all about this fucking war."

He slammed a loaded magazine into the P-38 he had just cleaned, quickly pulled back the carriage and let it slam forward with a sharp impact, and then immediately pulled the trigger.

The slug just barely grazed Morelli's ear, smashing into the wall behind his head with a deafening noise. Morelli turned white.

"You bastard, Brawley," he yelled out, jumping up and knocking over his chair as he pushed away from the table. "I'm not over here in this fucking, God-forsaken hell-hole just to be killed by some stupid bastard who doesn't know how to handle a pistol."

"Sorry, Morelli," Brawley said. "I forgot I put in a loaded magazine."

"Don't say another fucking word," Morelli said. "You can't explain away something that stupid. What you did is inexcusable."

Morelli left the room. I saw him standing in front of the house where it was probably safer in spite of the machine gun fire, the artillery shells, and the mortars.

It took about six hours for our own mortars and artillery to force the Germans to pull back from the bluff along the river, allowing our line companies to get enough men across to make it safe for the rest of the troops.

A few hours later, our platoon crossed over in boats. We waited on the other side, while the combat engineers laid a pontoon bridge across the river. Our jeeps were driven across and we were ready to head for Straubing.

It took us two days to reach the outskirts of Straubing. We had been reconnoitering the approaches to that town with very little resistance. The road suddenly veered to the left and as we turned, we were met with a volley of shots coming from the woods up ahead. We dove from the jeeps into the ditches. We were fairly sure that the firing came from a group of random snipers that were determined to get a few of us and then surrender. We returned their fire sporadically, whenever we could see any movement at the edge of the woods, but their fire kept us pinned down fairly effectively.

Charley Company, 1st Battalion was a few kilometers behind us, but we weren't able to contact them by radio.

"Now, let's not do anything stupid or heroic," Brawley said. "Charley Company will be here anytime now and we can wait the snipers out."

Even though our jeeps were standing in the middle of the road, the point men came around the bend without taking proper precautions and were immediately picked off by the snipers. There was an exchange of fire for about fifteen minutes. This suddenly stopped as if by prearrangement. It was very quiet after the shooting. There was no wind and nothing moved.

The snipers then started walking out of the woods with their hands on their heads, slowly crossing the field in very slow, tentative steps. There were six of them. It was still very quiet, not a sound, not a breeze. The Germans kept walking toward us, stopping, talking, and then starting again.

There were four dead rifle men from Charley Company lying in the sun on the edge of the road. I had a tight feeling in my chest and I was trying to hold my breath. My right hip began to ache where it pressed against a rock in the ground, but I didn't move.

The Germans stopped in the middle of the field, standing there motionless with their hands on their heads, undecided whether to continue on toward us or just to wait for us to make a move. I had a bead on one of them in the peep sights of my M1. They were about two hundred yards away. I saw them looking at one another and then back to us. Time seemed to have stopped.

The firing started just as suddenly as it had stopped before, as if one giant finger was pulling on all those triggers. No prisoners were taken that day.

Chapter 10

Food, Kaputt, and Banquets

The main fuel our platoon depended on besides gasoline was coffee. It was our life's blood. Every few minutes we had between missions and even during missions, if we could think of some reasonable excuse, which wasn't difficult to do, we would brew up some good strong coffee. With the British troops, we understood it was tea. With us, it was coffee, which was more important than ammunition.

When we started at Bitche, we were forced to eat K rations. That was all that was available at the OP. This was food without any taste. At least we were told it was food. After trying it, we weren't so sure. Our taste buds told us a different story.

The K ration for breakfast consisted of absolutely unpalatable, ground-up eggs and potatoes. For lunch, that package had cheese and crackers. It was impossible to recognize the cheese as cheese except by the printing on the box. I had never eaten cheese before that had no taste whatsoever. For supper, there was a tin of a substance identified as meat, a fruit bar, and a small package of bouillon powder. We never made any bouillon because it made us too thirsty, but we found out quickly that sprinkling it on the rest of the food made those items reasonably savory.

Occasionally, we managed to get some C rations, but this was rare. These were canned foods that were fairly tasty. We assumed that the rear echelon commandos kept them for themselves, just like all the rest of the things we were supposed to get but never did.

About once a week, we were able to get back to the company area for a hot meal. About three weeks after we had been in combat, we were especially hungry and tired. We needed a rest and some good, hot food. We drove back to the company area and stood in line, mess kits at the ready, smacking our lips because of the wonderful smell of all that delicious food just waiting to be eaten.

We couldn't believe what we heard as we stood in line. The mess sergeant was telling Sgt. Brawley that he wasn't authorized to serve us.

Brawley looked like he was ready to explode. His lip went out a mile.

"Why not?" he growled. "Are we the fucking enemy?"

"You don't have your 71st Division patches on your helmets, that's why," the cook said, his arms folded like a barricade against his chest. "Sgt. Colombresi gave us explicit orders not to serve anyone without the 71st patch. No patch, no chow."

"Why that fucking little son-of-a-bitch," Brawley said. "We ought to shoot that little bastard. Where the hell do we get the patches?"

"Don't ask me," the cook said. "I only work here. Now if you guys from the I and R Platoon fall out of line, I'll finish serving the rest of the men who have been behaving and have their patches on like good little boys."

"Well, of all the chickenshit outfits I've seen in this man's army," Brawley boomed out, "this takes the fucking cake."

We later found out that Patton had sent the order out. We also were instructed to apply seven layers of shellac to our helmet liners just as he had.

It took us about another half an hour to round up the company clerk and the supply sergeant to get the patches, take off the netting on our helmets, glue on the patches, replace the netting and finally, get back in the chow line.

Fortunately, Colombresi was nowhere in sight, having discreetly vanished when he heard the commotion. Without a doubt, he would have been our first Headquarters Company casualty.

The meals that we really looked forward to were the ones we prepared ourselves, with food scavenged from abandoned houses.

"Don't eat any of the food you find lying around these houses," Brawley had warned. "It might be poisoned."

That same day, we came into a house where there was a five-gallon tank of fresh milk on the floor, just taken from the cows that morning. There were two loaves of dark bread on the table. The milk and the bread disappeared very quickly. We didn't drop dead so Brawley had his share, too.

Another time, we collected six hundred eggs. We hardboiled the whole bunch. That came to thirty eggs per man. There was plenty of farting over the next twenty-four hours.

Our most elaborate meals consisted of fresh chicken that we caught in various coops throughout our mission area, plus any canned goods that we found in the abandoned houses. These banquets would take a good three hours to prepare. Lieut. Rickey, our great leader who was ignored by everyone in the platoon, would usually come back from making his intelligence reports only to find us in the middle of our dinner preparations.

After several of these elaborate banquets, the lieutenant became very annoyed because of the delay in starting our next mission. He acted as if we were deliberately slowing down the war, which we were, at least our part of it.

"From now on," he said, very emphatically, "there will be no more banquet-style coffee breaks. These have completely gotten out of hand. When I leave to make my reports to S2, you men will remain on the ready. You will be limited to brewing up some coffee and nothing more. I repeat, *and nothing more.* That's all. Do you all understand these simple instructions?"

Brawley muttered something under his breath.

"You have a question, Sgt. Brawley?" Lieut. Rickey asked coldly.

"No, not at the present time, sir, but I will have something to say regarding this problem sometime soon. You can bet on it."

It usually took Lieut. Rickey about two hours to make his standard report to S2, regimental intelligence, headed by Major Booker. During that time, he would also get his new destination target. All of us were suspicious about the length of time he required. The fact that he never appeared hungry when he came back also contributed to our distrust.

After an especially short reconnaissance one day, Lieut. Rickey again admonished us about any fancy dinner plans that we might be planning in his absence. He gave us a stern look as he drove off in one of the jeeps to make his report to S2.

"Morelli," Brawley called out as soon as Rickey was out of sight. "Follow that son-of-a-bitch from Utah. Get back here as soon as you can and tell me every move he makes."

Morelli took off like a jack rabbit to do his scouting, while Brawley gathered everybody around him for the next phase of our plans.

"Now listen, this is going to be the biggest goddamned blast ever seen on the Western Front. If we do it right, they'll be talking about this in all the divisions in the European Theater of War. Bill Mauldin might even draw a cartoon commemorating this day. So scatter out and grab everything that can be eaten. We'll rendezvous here between thirty and sixty minutes, depending how successful you are. So get your skinny asses moving."

"What about the Lieutenant's warning about no more fancy dinner breaks, Sergeant Brawley?" one of the men asked.

"Fuck the Lieutenant," Brawley said scornfully. "He warned us about fancy dinner breaks, but he never said a word about the biggest fucking dinner break ever seen in this war, did he?"

Everybody was in a good mood by then, laughing and joking. By the time the men started drifting back with their arms full, chickens clucking, Morelli also pulled in, tires screeching as he slammed on the breaks.

"It's just what you thought, Sergeant," he said, out of breath. "That son-of-a-bitch is with Major Booker and they're both digging into the biggest goddamn steak I ever saw anywhere. They're drinking wine, besides. I was drooling all the way back here with the smell of that steak in my nose. While I was scouting around, I managed to pick up this case of canned goods from the kitchen."

He took out a carton from the jeep and put it with all the other stuff the men had found.

"Good work, Morelli," Brawley said. "Our suspicions were right on target. We'll fix the bastard this time, once and for all, even if it sets the war back three days."

There were ten chickens in all, fifty eggs, six loaves of dark bread, several jars of venison and a variety of vegetables, plus the cans Morelli commandeered. The fires were roaring, the water boiling, and all the men were busy when Lieut. Rickey drove back about thirty minutes later.

He took one look at us and nearly became hysterical. His voice went up a full octave and he started to yell like a madman, his arms going back and forth like a broken-down windmill.

"Stop what you're doing immediately and get into your vehicles," he hollered. "I'll give you ten seconds to haul your asses out of here."

His face was the color of a Sherman tank just blasted into flames by a direct hit.

We didn't even turn around to acknowledge his presence. We bent over whatever we were doing. Most of us were plucking and cleaning chickens.

"Hand me that pot over there, Lieutenant," Brawley yelled over his shoulder. He didn't bother to turn around, either.

"Has everybody gone deaf?" the Lieutenant roared. "You have exactly ten seconds to drop everything you're doing and get into your jeeps."

He looked at his watch to time us. Brawley handed him a chicken with its head cut off and still twitching.

"Start plucking, Lieutenant Rickey, or sit your ass down," Brawley intoned. "The other day you asked me if I had anything to say about your decision to limit our breaks to coffee breaks only. Today you're going to get my answer. This is it: I don't want to hear another word out of your mouth until we're done with our dinner. You were caught red-handed eating steak with Major Booker at the officer's mess and drinking wine, besides. You're a fine son-of-a-bitch to tell us not to eat. Men have been shot for less than that. So if you want to get back into the good graces of the men in this platoon, I suggest that you start plucking, Lieutenant, just start plucking."

Lieut. Rickey sat down and started to pluck. Morelli had put a pot of boiling water between his feet. He never uttered another word throughout the meal. When everybody had finished eating, we sat around emitting exaggerated belches and rubbing our bellies, congratulating ourselves on a stupendous meal.

Lieut. Rickey watched us silently, a pained expression on his face. He finally said in a low voice, as we put the last pieces of equipment away, "Are you men ready now?"

Sgt. Brawley looked him straight in the eye and said, "You can go to your jeep now and mount up, Lieutenant."

From that moment on, there was no longer any question of who our leader was. Lieut. Rickey never warned us again about preparing elaborate meals during our breaks. He even started eating with the men to show us he was a regular guy. If General Patton ever wondered what slowed up the war that day in April, 1945, he never bothered to mention it to anybody.

It was shortly after that memorable dinner that we all began to refer to Lieut. Rickey as "Kaputt". We gave him that nickname because he had led us through a German mine field where safe paths hadn't yet been laid out by the combat engineers. He was totally unaware of what he'd just done. By coincidence, he had his driver stop on the way back next to the large white sign with black print, warning us not to drive past the markers. He sat there looking sweet and innocent, not yet knowing why we were so upset with him. Miraculously, not one mine had been tripped. After that, Sgt. Brawley advised him to stay in the third jeep of the patrol except when we neared the company area in the rear, where he again could take the lead and play soldier.

Just past Fulda on April 5, we drove through a small town that had a brewery. Unfortunately, every barrel had a bullet hole in it except one that Morelli, by exceptionally diligent search, found deep in the bowels of the building.

There was a warehouse full of Norwegian sardines down the street and we proceeded to drink the keg dry and eat as many tins of sardines as our stomachs could hold. Five did it for me. Morelli beat me out with six. In Meningen, which we occupied on April 7, we found another warehouse that was full of French champagne. We drank it every night for a week, celebrating the fact that we had gotten through another day completely intact.

All in all, the war seemed to be progressing very well. We were very happy that the Germans kept retreating in full flight. This certainly made our lives easier.

Chapter 11

Madame Angele deVivre

Morelli and I fell in love with Madame Angele deVivre as soon as we met her that day in St. Laurent en Caux. And she loved us right back. That was the kind of woman she was. There was something transmitted in the air, something extremely subtle, a chemical transmutation, an electromagnetism, that a man was aware of as soon as he was within fifty feet of her radiant beauty. Your whole body would immediately stand at attention, front and center. Your vital member, proudly firm and erect, throbbing with anticipation and ready to serve its master at a moment's notice, no matter what the cost, the one organ you valued even more than your arm or leg, would instantly point to the North Star.

Well, she quickly became the star in our firmament and it was through mere chance that Morelli and I got to know her.

One week after landing in France, before hitting the front at Bitche, we went into St. Laurent en Caux, the small village adjacent to our staging area, to do a little exploring and to try out some of the French cuisine, having gotten tired of regular army food like Spam and SOS (chipped beef in a thick fat sauce spread on a hard piece of toast that army men called "Shit on a Shingle"). There was only one restaurant in the entire village. It was completely unpretentious, with about a dozen neat and clean tables, all covered with red and white checkered tablecloths.

The waiter, a short individual with a little Charlie Chaplin mustache (or was it an Adolf Hitler mustache?) came out of the kitchen and stopped suddenly, standing there looking at us, rather surprised.

We were not supposed to fraternize with the French at that time.

"Gentlemen," he said, clearing his throat several times. "What can I do for you?"

"Ah, you speak English," I said. "That is very good."

"But, of course," he said proudly, smoothing out his mustache with the side of his forefinger. "This is a small village, but there are a certain enlightened few in these environs who speak English, and of course German, which we were forced to learn during the occupation. To survive we do what we must do."

"What is the specialty of the house, garçon?"

"Our specialty of the house, messieurs," he said, clearing his throat, his eyes going up to the ceiling, "is lapin, that is to say, rabbit, or as they say in learned circles, 'Leporidae'. We used to serve, before the war and during the subsequent occupation by les boches, pork, beef, chicken, and lamb, but what the Germans could not confiscate, the local farmers now hoard. So we make the best of a poor situation and serve rabbit. And if I do not catch any of my furry friends in my traps tonight, we will not even have that to serve tomorrow."

"We shall have rabbit, then, garçon," Morelli said. "And what do you suggest to drink? My friend and I have a terrible fire in our throats."

"Ah, there, messieurs, we do have a truly authentic specialty of the house. It is a local drink which is not well known outside of the province of Normandy. It is called Calvados. I must warn you though, that it, indeed, is very powerful. It will replace the fire of thirst in your throats with the fire of a remarkable liquid. The other soldiers before you called it 'white lightning,' for its ability to stir your passions to a frenzy, but at the same time, rob you of your power. It also works quite well in your cigarette lighters, I've been told by many American fighting men."

"Then it will be Calvados for each of us, garçon," I said.

"Why not?" Morelli said. "After all, this is a special occasion."

"And the special occasion, messieurs?" the waiter asked, his eyebrows up a notch. "What exactly is it, if I may be so bold as to ask?"

"The French Revolution," Morelli said, with a straight face.

"We are celebrating the one-hundred-and-fifty-sixth year since the great rebellion against that rascal, Louis XVI, and by God, we're going to let it all hang out."

While we were drinking our first Calvados in honor of the French Revolution, feeling it burn its fiery path to our stomachs, Madame Angele deVivre spied us through the window and came in like a burst of sunshine on a rainy day. She permeated the area with a delicate mist of perfume that enraptured us that very moment. She was a ravishing woman of about forty, gorgeous beyond description, provocative, amply endowed with a beautiful, overflowing bosom, flashing dark eyes, and a magnificently contoured behind that she knew exactly how to swing in the most maddening way. Every part of my body came to full military attention and I discovered, at that moment in time, the exact location of true north, my anatomical pointer indicating that specific direction and already quivering in anticipation of studying an unusual celestial body in all its radiant glory, sequestered deep in a remote village in Normandy.

"My dear sweet boys," she said in a soft throaty voice with a delicious French accent, "I am Madame Angele deVivre, and I am so overjoyed to meet the great liberators of our glorious France. I couldn't resist coming in to tell you this. I just can't show my appreciation enough."

She hummed and twirled with her arms extended and Morelli and I began to sweat. We both thought, was it the fire of the Calvados or this wondrous woman that caused this remarkable reaction?

She bent over us and revealed the full magnificence of her breasts, nestled so serenely inside her clinging silk dress, seemingly aching to burst forth from their confinement. And again that soft delicate fragrance wafted over us and Morelli and I nearly swooned. There was no doubt that we were completely mesmerized.

"The Calvados is very strong, messieurs," the waiter said, observing Morelli and me with a keen eye.

He cleared his throat several times as if trying to break the spell we were under.

"It weakens your resistance and resolution," he continued, "and you must practice a certain amount of diligence and restraint."

Madame deVivre ignored him and so did we.

"You must come to our farm on the edge of the village," she continued, humming snatches of a Strauss waltz in between her words. "My husband will slaughter a pig for the occasion and I shall prepare some crêpes and we shall all have such a splendid time dancing, singing, and whatever else you boys can think of."

And with that, she crushed Morelli's face to her bosom, his nose getting the full benefit of that glorious anatomical masterpiece. She then hummed and waltzed over to me.

"Oh, Madame deVivre, we certainly shall come to your farm," I said, my voice suddenly muffled by those prodigious, globular attributes, as she hugged me in turn.

"Nothing can stop us, I assure you, Madame," Morelli added, just to seal the deal.

She gave us directions to her home, saying she would expect us the very next night at six o'clock. As quickly as she had swept in, she was gone, a brilliant, humming, shooting star that ignited all of our sexual fantasies. She left behind a faint scent of wild mountain flowers that hovered in the air and gently wafted into our noses.

We had another Calvados each, finished the rabbit, which was excellent, and then staggered off to our cold pyramidal tents, our canvas cots, our piss cans and our dreams, heads swimming. We wondered if Madame deVivre was a result of too much Calvados and a joint dream that Morelli and I somehow dreamt together. We sang all the way back to the company area that old English hymn of desire on the Western Front: "Roll me over, in the clover, roll me over, lay me down, and do it again."

The next day, Morelli and I gathered together some soap, toothpaste, candy, cigarettes, tobacco, and coffee, and presented ourselves promptly at six o'clock at Madame deVivre's house.

"Oh, you dear, sweet boys," she hummed and sang. "How very thoughtful of you. You are so kind to bring all these gifts. Thank you, thank you so much. Vous êtes trés gentil, merci. How can I ever show you my deep appreciation? But wait until you see the feast I have prepared for you."

Our eyes had already feasted on that divine body of hers. Now we knew she was real and not just a part of our dreams or the result of drinking too much Calvados. Morelli looked at me and I looked at

Morelli and our eyes rolled around like four loose marbles inside our heads.

She introduced us to her husband, Étienne, a quiet, gaunt man of very few words, puffing away at his pipe. He was obviously much older than his wife and wisely let her do most of the talking.

We had an elegant supper of roast pork, potatoes, carrots, corn, along with a superb white wine, followed by apple pie and coffee. That was the first decent meal we'd had in over two months. Monsieur deVivre then lit up his pipe with the tobacco we had given him and puffed himself into a cloud of blue smoke and oblivion, while Morelli and I helped our little angel clean up the dining room and wash all the dishes, pots, pans, and utensils.

Within twenty minutes or so, we were all sitting in the parlor and Madame deVivre looked at her husband and said politely, "Étienne, I believe you have some work to do in the barn, n'est pas?"

"Oui, ma cherie," he responded quickly, as though it had been all prearranged. He added something that I didn't catch, excused himself, put on his cap and departed, leaving a trail of aromatic tobacco smoke.

Madame deVivre went over to an old victrola standing in the corner of the room.

"My dear boys," she crooned, "I do hope both of you know how to dance because I am simply mad about dancing. As a young woman, I had some wild ideas about being a ballet dancer and I trained in Rouen for a year or so, but my father put an end to those dreams after my mother died. Now I don't have many opportunities to practice what I had learned during that short time."

She turned the crank on the old machine and put on a Strauss waltz and away we went, our heads swimming with the excitement of holding her so close. After a few waltzes, alternating with Morelli and me, she looked at us demurely and said, "Now if you boys sit here for a few moments, I will give you a special treat."

Before she left the room, she picked out another record and placed it on the victrola.

"Will one of you sweet boys start this record when I come back into the room?"

Morelli nearly fell over himself getting there in a rush. She patted him on the head, like a school teacher giving her approval to a student. She then slipped away into an adjoining room. Morelli looked at me and shrugged his shoulders, as if to say: "This woman is totally unpredictable, but interesting as all hell. What is she going to do next?"

Within a few minutes, we heard her sing out from the other room, "Are you boys ready?"

She sounded like a solo violin introduction.

She stepped back into the room with a shy curtsy as Morelli started the music. She was totally naked, her voluptuous body barely concealed by several transparent pink veils. She appeared completely relaxed and absorbed in her dance while Morelli and I watched her with our jaws gaping.

"I shall dance for you Salome's dance and then you dear, sweet boys must grant me any wish, just as Herod did when Salome asked for the head of John the Baptist for spurning her advances."

The music began with the agitation of kettle drums followed by the trumpet sounding briefly. "Ich will den koft des Jochanaan." I want the head of Jochanaan! There was a sudden burst of shrieking violins followed by the oboe, all with a tentative rhythm at first, the violins high in the background. As she turned and twisted, limbs extended, revealing the soft, delicate curve of the muscles of her calves, the lovely arch of her neck enhanced by a supplicating glance to the heavens, she slowly traced imaginary circles on the floor. It was a magnificent blending of motion and music. The veils parted as she moved, revealing the abrupt curve of her buttocks and the soft cupping of her umbilicus in the gentle swell of her belly and the dark shadow of her pubis. She was dancing out a reflection of Salome's real self, her unrevealed tenderness, her capability for deep love, and then again her uncontrolled desire for vengeance that overwhelmed her after her love was so contemptuously cast aside—her terrible despair, her entire being so delicately balanced on the edge of this cataclysmic inferno which drew nearer and nearer until in a moment of convulsive ecstasy and utter hopelessness, with the clarinets and piccolos joining in a deafening crescendo, her breasts in a sweet undulation with her erect nipples well demarcated indentations in the transparency of the veils, there were three sudden bursts of the coda and it was all over.

My heart was pounding and I could barely breathe. The veils had dropped away and she stood before me with tears in her eyes, a faint glistening moisture on her skin, beckoning me, arms extended, enticing me to rise from my chair and face my destiny like a man. Was I to meet the same fate as John the Baptist? If that was to be my destiny, I was ready. I slowly rose from the chair like a creature totally under the mystical spell of this angel from heaven, suddenly overwhelmed by a tremendous urge to reenter the womb where nineteen years before I had traveled a similar passage, exiting ignominiously butt first, apparently holding on for dear life, while the old doctor continued to pull laboriously, finally breaking my arm in the process, as I came out kicking, screaming, and squalling.

She gently took my hand and I followed her to my ineluctable rendezvous with destiny. There was no doubt in my mind at the time that this was truly Salome.

"We won't be long, you dear, sweet boy," she sang out to Morelli as the harsh scratching of the victrola needle gradually brought me back to reality. "There is enough of Salome for the two of you."

With that, she closed the door to the small door where she had first donned her veils. She stretched out languorously on the bed and let out a long sigh.

"Now you can guess my wish, can't you?" she said so quietly that I barely heard her.

I stood there transfixed, all my vital parts standing rigidly at attention, my heart pounding so strongly that I was afraid it would burst through my chest wall. I was fully prepared to be sacrificed on the altar of love.

"You dear, sweet boy," she said as I approached her, her eyelids down demurely. "You have been in this rigid condition all evening, I noticed, and you have broken out in a terrible sweat. It is now time to provide you with some relief."

Thank God, I thought, that Richard Strauss didn't drag Salome's dance out any longer.

She undressed me.

"Such a lovely thing," she whispered as she fell back with

another long sigh, helping me so thoughtfully in overcoming my nervous clumsiness.

Together we soared into the heavens, my auto pilot fixated on the North Star. After circling that heavenly body, we started a slow, floating descent back to earth. I was absolutely convinced that Benjamin Franklin was right in his advice to a young man. There was nothing like an older woman to be your tutor, especially if she could play the part of Salome.

There was a long silence while our hearts resumed their normal rhythm.

"My dear, sweet boy, you have performed well. I assume that this is the first time you have been exposed to Salome's dance. Just a few more lessons and undoubtedly, you will be a virtuoso. Now if you'll excuse me for a few minutes while I freshen up, I shall be ready for that other sweet boy."

After Salome's second dance, we all sat in the parlor, fully dressed and limp from the arduous task she had demanded of us, our heads still intact.

Madame deVivre looked at us kindly and said, "Could you have imagined a more pleasant evening, my dear, sweet boys?"

She settled herself comfortably on the couch between Morelli and me, her hands resting on our thighs. It was just like being plugged into an electric socket.

"I can see that you boys are ready for another rendition of Salome's dance. Ah, there is nothing like youth, but it takes a mature woman to know how to enjoy it. But tonight, you must forgive me. Je suis très fatiguée. Dancing is so tiring, especially if you put your whole heart and soul into it like I do. But by tomorrow night, if you arrive at seven o'clock sharp, we shall have crêpes and then a repeat performance. I shall dance Salome's dance once again and again the two of you shall grant me my wish. Poor Étienne is too old and can no longer grant me any of my wishes. He suffers from an excess of sugar, the poor dear, which has robbed him of all his passion and power. But he is so understanding."

She kissed both of us.

"You must remember one thing," she said. "Everything on this earth is so temporary, that sooner than we expect, we become mere spectators in this life and we are left with nothing but our memories."

She kissed us both again, leaving us at the door with that same faint scent of wild mountain flowers. Morelli and I drifted to the company area on a million clouds. We walked slowly in the dark, not wanting the magic of the night to end.

"Wouldn't it be nice if all women were as wise as Madame deVivre and made such simple demands of men?" I said on the way back.

"I think we just experienced a moment in heaven," Morelli answered.

For three straight weeks, we were in heaven with Madame deVivre from seven to ten o'clock every evening, while her husband worked in the barn. Morelli and I became experts on the music of Richard Strauss and Salome's dance as interpreted by that lovely lady. Like a true artist, she added little variations every night that kept us enthralled with anticipation.

We finally got our military orders to move out. We didn't know where we were going, but we knew we were going to relieve some battle-weary division somewhere on the front.

"We'll soon be leaving for the front, Madame," I said that final week in St. Laurent en Caux, not worried at all about the possibility of her being a spy, even though she danced to German music.

"Yes, I fear for you two sweet boys," Madame deVivre said in a trembling voice. "As soon as I train you to enjoy Salome's dance, you are taken away. But remember what I told you, that's what life is really all about, just one brief moment on the earth and then poof, it is over."

Tears welled up in her eyes.

"I must stop this," she said, dabbing at her eyes with her handkerchief, "because I am already crying."

Her beautiful dark eyes were puffy and red.

"If there is any last wish that we can grant you, Madame, please tell us now," I said, being ready, as usual, for any sacrifice.

We knew her cupboard was overflowing. Étienne had enough tobacco to last him a lifetime and Madame deVivre had enough soap, candy, chocolates, toothpaste, salt, sugar, and cigarettes to open a grocery store.

"Étienne will be gone for three days," she said, "traveling to Rouen on farm business to buy and trade some cattle and horses. I would like you dear, sweet boys to be with me as much as possible during that time. We shall think of some new games that we can play together, the three of us, à trois, as they say. Of course, that is after I perform Salome's dance, you understand. I am utterly useless as a woman unless I first perform my dance."

When it was all over that last night, we all cried. Even Étienne joined us in that activity. But in our hearts, no matter how sad we felt, we knew that Madame deVivre would soon find somebody new to dance for, some other dear, sweet boys who would be willing to grant her wish, and forever remember her as we did, the reincarnation of Salome, truly an angel from heaven.

The next morning we piled into two-and-a-half ton trucks, headed for Bitche, France, east of Nancy and close to the German border, with the Maginot line facing the Siegfried line, where weary, frightened men gathered in a fierce determination to kill one another, a billion light years away from a beautiful celestial body, the Polar Star, and Madame Angele deVivre.

Chapter 12

Ba-ba-balls

I saw Ba-ba-balls for the last time in the border town of Braunau, Austria, on May 1, 1945. Early in the morning there had been a
light snow, but later the sun came out and it turned into a beautiful
spring day. We didn't expect any significant resistance or even any
contact with the Germans at that point, but as our platoon approached
the dam there, we heard the angry cracking of machine gun bullets as
they snapped just over our heads. Morelli jammed on the brakes and
all of us jumped out of the jeeps into the ditch along the road. I had
the radio ear phones clipped to my helmet and plugged into the set
when I jumped. Luckily, I didn't have my chin strap on because my
helmet was ripped off my head as though I had been struck by a
baseball bat. For a moment I thought that I had been hit by a Mauser
8mm round. I lay in the ditch rubbing my neck for a few moments,
while the others started to crawl up the hill toward the dam.

The Germans had the entire area covered with machine gun fire
and, periodically, they would pull out an 88 from somewhere, fire the
big gun like a rifle, and then hide the damn thing again before we
could even see what they were up to. It certainly didn't appear as
though we'd be getting across the dam anytime soon.

We were pinned down for about an hour before we got some
help from three of the tanks attached to our regiment. They unloaded
a few 76mm rounds from their new guns while the machine gunners
went to town, preventing the Germans from using their hidden 88.
Within thirty minutes, the Germans decided they had had enough
excitement for one day. They filed across the dam with their hands on

top of their heads. I was standing by the lead tank and nearly dropped my drawers in shock as I saw Ba-ba-balls jump out of the turret. I was just about to call to him, happy as hell to see him, when he caught two rounds in the chest from a lone, determined sniper on the other side of the dam. I ran over just as Ba-ba fell off the Sherman, coughing up blood. I caught him and lowered him gently to the ground. Our medic, Doc Newman, came over. He took one look and shook his head.

"J-J-Jesus Christ," Ba-ba said gasping, blood pouring out of his mouth.

"Hang on, Ba," I said. "The ambulance is just down the road."

"Ba-ba-balls," Ba-ba said. "You know I'll never make it, Zeb, so don't try to kid me. I was going to tell you how good it was to see you when that f-f-fucker caught me in the chest."

He spoke haltingly, spitting out blood.

"Bullshit, Ba," I said. "I'm not trying to kid you, buddy. You can't die on me now. If you go, I have to go, too. Remember, we do everything together, just like we did down by the river when we were kids."

His fingers were digging into my arm and I could feel him losing his strength. He was breathing with difficulty and his face was distorted with pain. He was going fast and it was killing me.

I was crying openly now.

"You can't die, Ba," I said. "Do you hear me? I'll never forgive you if you do, you son-of-a-bitch. Remember, you're the grand champion pisser of all times."

He started to whisper something, trying to smile. I could barely hear him. I bent down close to his mouth.

"You're the grand champion pisser now, Zeb," he said softly.

He coughed up some more blood and then with a long sigh, closed his eyes and slumped over dead in my arms.

His captain was awarded a silver star for that action even though he was five hundred yards behind us. Ba-ba was awarded a body bag.

I can still see him lying there beside the big Sherman, blood oozing out of his mouth, all the men standing around in the bright sunlight watching him die.

But I prefer to remember him the way he was when we were

growing up, farting around the old Indian Trail along the Connecticut River, out-drinking and out-pissing me, declaring his supremacy over all the other pissers of the world, atop a rough boulder, arms outstretched, his words sailing out on their own slippery sea of saliva and still echoing in my brain over all these years.

****

It was difficult being a close friend of Ba-ba-balls Loudry because of the juicy way he had of speaking. Even at twelve feet, you could feel the projectiles of saliva pepper your face when he got really excited. And I guess I was just about his closest friend within the twelve-foot radius. If you dared to come closer than twelve feet, your nose would soon look like the prow of some beleaguered ship tossed about on the high seas, dripping with spit until a huge glob collected at the tip and dropped off to splash on your shoes.

It was funny, too, because I remember long hours of practicing in front of a mirror, trying to imitate his exact way of speaking until my image disappeared in a gooey, salivary mess and I still never managed to attain the perfect consistency of his speech.

Each of his words seemed swathed in its own cocoon of saliva, and he frequently assumed the royal arrogance of King Louis of France when speaking to his friends. But lurking behind this facade could be seen the sly smile of the devil overcoming his features after letting loose with an especially brilliant salvo.

His real name was Camille, which he hated. So we called him Camel for awhile, which he also hated. He got his nickname from his stuttering. His favorite retort to everything was "Balls," but when he said it, the word always came out "Ba-ba-balls." And in time, that's what we ended up calling him, "Ba-ba-balls."

Occasionally, we shortened this to "Ba-ba." But only his closest friends dared to go one step further and call him "Ba."

And when I said "Ba," he would stop and listen no matter what he was doing because he knew in his heart that I was the only one in our gang who would venture to stand within a two foot radius and defy his rapid-fire mouth that spewed out microscopic spitballs at the unimaginable rate of five thousand a second.

That's the way it was that day on the old Indian Trail between the New York, New Haven and Hartford railroad tracks and the Connecticut River in Enfield, Connecticut, not far from where we lived. It was hot with the sun boiling down on us in a cloudless sky. There wasn't a breath of air to evaporate the sweat that rolled down our faces. We had just finished playing a game of baseball down at the old vacant lot at the end of Spring Street and we were sitting there resting on a log.

"Do you hear the falls across the tracks, Ba?" I asked.

"Y-y-yeah," Ba-ba said, stretching out his entire length on the grass, his eyes shut against the sun. He knew what was on my mind because we had done this many times before.

"The Well is a hop, skip, and a jump from the falls, Ba, and I'm ready to challenge you again."

The Well was a fifty foot outcropping of red shale along the river. At its base was a bubbling spring of ice-cold water.

"And you see what I brought along with me, Ba?" I said, holding up a small empty bottle.

He turned to look, putting his hand up to shade his eyes.

"I-I-I can see you've been planning, Zeb," he said, "and so soon after your last defeat. Y-y-you're a real sucker for punishment."

"That's right, Ba," I said. "I'm going to keep trying until I win. You'd better loosen your belt."

"I-I-I don't have to loosen my belt until after the first g-g-gallon, Zeb. You know that from past experience. And after I beat you drinking the spring water, I'll outpiss you by t-t-three feet as always."

And the saliva came in a stream in anticipation of the challenge. Perhaps that was the reason he could always beat me. He was like an old, leaky steam engine that constantly needed a fresh supply of water to maintain a head of steam.

We sat at the edge of the spring cross-legged as the contest began. There was no fooling and no joking. This was serious business. I was determined to beat Ba-ba this time. I hadn't had anything to drink since the night before in preparation for this battle.

One bottle after another went down the hatch, first Ba-ba, and then me. He went first, being the champion. Ba-ba would wipe his mouth after drinking his bottle of water, emitting a long drawn-out "Ahhhhh" to indicate his deep satisfaction, while attempting to undermine my confidence at the same time. Like all contests, there was a big psychological factor here and Ba-ba used all the tricks he could think of. He'd hand the bottle to me in a rather cavalier fashion, as if to indicate how utterly hopeless my attempt to beat him would be.

Our stomachs gradually began to protrude in front of our backbones like two monstrous sacks that gurgled as we moved. We sat there like two fat toads, bellies stretched tight by the internal pressure of all that water.

I finally gave up.

"I can't take another drop, Ba-ba," I gasped, the water dripping out of my mouth, my bladder up around my ears.

"S-s-so, you had enough, Zeb," Ba-ba said.

With a triumphant swoop, followed by a loud Indian yell, he refilled the bottle and slugged down the entire contents once again, looking as if he had been stranded on a desert island for two weeks.

He stood up, arms extended to the sky, his monstrous belly protruding like a bloated bag, his knickers down around his ankles, yelling out for the whole world to hear: "Still the world champion spring water drinker of all time."

He let out another blood-curdling yell, beating his fists against his chest. He flung the bottle against the stones along the river, smashing it into a million pieces and then sat down.

"Ba-ba," I said solemnly, "I bow to you. But next time you have to promise not to talk during the contest, because when you talk it's like spitting, and that's like a leak in your water tank, so then you have more room for more water."

"Rise, Zeb," Ba-ba said, his voice swelling to a regal pitch. "No matter what the rules are, I have confidence that I shall win."

He pulled himself up to his feet with some difficulty.

"N-n-now let's proceed to the pissing arena where I shall again demonstrate that I can outpiss you or anyone else and p-p-prove once more that I am the greatest pisser in the world."

Our pissing arena was fifty yards down the river from the spring, a sandy area where we had left our marks in the sand, relieving the bursting pressure in our bladders after previous contests. As we walked there, unable to bend because of the vast expanse of our bellies, while hearing the water slosh inside our stomachs, I looked at

Ba-ba. He was grinning from ear to ear, supremely sure of himself, as usual. He had every reason to be confident. After all, he had won every contest since we had started dueling in the sand.

"I'll try again, Ba-ba," I said, "even though I think I already know the outcome of this contest."

"Y-y-you're a good loser, Zeb, and I know you never give up without a fight. And remember, y-y-you're probably the second-best pisser in the whole world and that's nothing to sneeze at."

We arrived at the pissing arena and Ba-ba climbed up on a large boulder, our pissing rock, grunting and groaning as he maneuvered his big belly up its slippery surface.

"H-h-hear ye, hear ye, all you grand and hopeful pissers of the world. Gather around for the greatest pissing duel known to man."

I stepped forward, rod in hand pointing directly south toward Windsor Locks.

Ba-ba took out a small pocket compass, tested the direction of the wind, pointed himself exactly south by southeast, and with a mighty terrifying Indian yell, let loose a prodigious stream of urine that arced brilliantly in the sun, splintering the light into a golden rainbow and landing in the sand well beyond his best distance yet.

"T-t-there you are, Zeb," he said triumphantly. "Beat that if you can."

"Holy shit, Ba-ba," I yelled out. "You didn't have to go and break your old record, did you?"

But just at that moment, I felt a sudden breeze on my skinny little ass, having previously ascended the rock to stand by Ba-ba, and catching the wind exactly right, let loose with my mightiest endeavor yet. It landed one foot short of Ba-ba's marks, but well beyond his old record.

Out of the corner of my eye, I saw Ba-ba lean forward with his mouth wide open and his eyes bulging.

"J-J-Jesus, Zeb, you beat my old record by a foot and you nearly out-pissed me. You caught that breeze on your ass just right. I'll have to give you credit for that and watch you very carefully in the future,"

That's the way it always was with Ba-ba, a true champion in every sense of the word.

"Ba-ba, I'm not kidding. I really think you'll go down in history as the biggest pisser the world has ever known, even bigger than Benjamin Franklin."

"Y-y-you're right, Zeb. I don't think anybody can beat me at this stage of my career. I didn't know Benjamin Franklin was a big pisser. They don't teach you that in the history books. But I'd better make my marks in the sand now because when I get to be as old as my old man, I'll probably be pissing down my leg into my left shoe."

"You should be in the Olympics, Ba-ba," I said. "That's where you should be, a gold medal winner."

"You'd be right next to me with a silver medal, Zeb."

Ba-ba lived on South River street and I lived in an old white house at the end of Thompson Court. The railroad tracks were in a depression between us. Thompsonville was unique in a sense, because even though we both lived on opposite sides of the railroad, we both lived on the "wrong" side of the tracks. We were the poorest of the poor. But we weren't aware of this fact so it never bothered us. In fact, we thought everybody was poor.

Once a week on Sunday night at 8:30 p.m., the Washington-Boston train would stop at the station in Thompsonville. The last car was always a balcony car and it would be just about even with the ninety-degree turn Thompson Court took as it veered away from the tracks.

Bill, a tall, lanky gray-haired black man was always there waiting for us on the balcony, smiling and waving to us.

"How many you boys out there tonight?" he'd say.

"Six, Bill," we'd all yell out.

"OK," Bill would say, handing us a bag. "Here are three apples and three oranges. I threw in a few cookies, too. Now be careful 'cause the train is just about ready to pull out of the station. So long, boys. See you next week."

"Thanks, Bill," we'd yell out after him as the train gradually pulled away, the whistle blowing.

He stood there on the balcony, smiling and waving to us.

Bill knew that was the only fruit we had all week. We never knew his last name or where he came from, but as far as Ba-ba and I and the other kids were concerned, Bill came from heaven, a black angel.

It was 1933.

Every summer on the day school ended, my second oldest brother, Walt, would give us baseball caps and take us over to old man Fogarty's house for our annual baldy haircuts. Fogarty was a retired barber who gave all the kids baldies "for free." He felt it was his contribution to the health of our society and demonstrated his personal dedication to stop the spread of lice.

I remember Ba-ba looking confused when I told him I was getting a baldy that first time. After I explained my brother's simple logic, no hair, no lice, he decided to go along with me and get one himself. After all, the idea of not having to comb your hair or even wash your head all summer was an enticing one. After old man Fogarty finished with me, Ba-ba had to lie on the floor from the stomach cramps he got from laughing so much.

"You look awfully funny, Zeb," he said. "I never knew your ears stuck out so far. I bet you can wiggle them."

He got a baldy, too, just to prove what a good friend he was. Then I was on the floor laughing. I think that's the reason old man Fogarty enjoyed cutting everybody's hair off. He stood there laughing, too.

"Not only do your ears stick out as much as mine, Ba-ba," I said, "but your nose looks longer now that your hair's gone."

Ba-ba looked in the mirror and put on his baseball cap immediately.

"A lot of people are going to be laughing at us skinheads this summer," he said, giggling, flipping his cap sideways and making a comical face.

We then went over to my house where my mother gave us each a small cloth bag with a square piece of camphor inside. We had to wear this all summer around our necks to prevent polio.

"You really thinks this works?" Ba-ba asked.

"Well, I never get a sore throat and I never had polio," I said.

"That's good enough for me," Ba-ba said.

That was one thing that could be said about Ba-ba: he never doubted simple, clear logic and irrefutable scientific evidence.

Forty-five years later, I found out that camphor stimulates the immune system.

That summer, the older guys taught us how to smoke corn silk, old dried-up leaves, and just plain rolled-up newspaper. The trouble with newspaper cigarettes was the fact that they occasionally flamed up and singed our eyebrows. They never singed our hair because we didn't have any.

After one big flame-out, Ba-ba came up with a good idea. We each took an empty cigar box down to the entrance of the Bigelow Sanford Carpet Company on Main Street. We collected all the butts the men threw down as they entered the factory. When we had a good supply, we went down the railroad tracks past the falls where there was a water conduit beneath the rails. We'd lean up against the curved brick wall with our feet planted on the opposite side and smoke until we got sick to our stomachs and vomited. That's what made us give up smoking the first time, Ba-ba and I, at the ages of nine and eight respectively.

Ba-ba was thrown out of public school for being intractable. He then entered the sixth grade in St. Patrick's Parochial School where he proceeded to make the nuns' lives miserable from day one. I was in the fifth grade in Center School at the time. Fifth grade was actually half-fifth and half-sixth, both halves in one room taught by a pleasant lady named Miss White. Ba-ba wasn't really a bad kid in the real sense of the word as we understand it today. He just couldn't keep his big mouth shut at certain times and this usually got him into a fair amount of trouble. Like the time he told the fifth-grade teacher, Mr. Angelica, to go piss up a tree.

"What did you say, young man?" Mr. Angelica asked, his face flushing. This was obviously the wrong question to ask. The whole class was giggling by then and Ba-ba was playing up to the audience.

"I-I-I said go piss up a tree," Ba-ba said.

"Get out of my classroom, Balls," Mr. Angelica said fuming, forgetting himself for a moment. "I mean Mr. Loudry," he added quickly. "And don't come back."

By then, the class was rolling in the aisles. They also knew they were in for piles of home work. Mr. Angelica wasn't known for his sense of humor.

In the parochial school, Ba-ba got many a crack across the knuckles with a ruler, swung with great enthusiasm by the nuns. This, too, had no effect on him. His mouth kept right on going, the spit flying.

When I turned nine, I went to work for Ba-ba to help him with his paper route. He figured I was mature enough at nine to handle money. He delivered the *Springfield Daily News* that was published in Springfield, Massachusetts, but had a big section devoted to north central Connecticut, which included Thompsonville.

Ba-ba had about seventy customers, having picked up about twenty new people since he acquired the route. This was too much to handle all by himself and that's when he asked me to work for him.

The paper cost two cents a copy. The total cost for one week was twelve cents because there was no Sunday delivery. Most of the people were good to us even though nobody had much money. It was 1934 when I started to work for Ba-ba, and it was surprising how many people would fork over fifteen cents a week, especially if we put the paper inside the screen door or folded it up between the door knob and the jamb. Of course, some of our customers were rotten eggs who never paid their bills. We had to pay the newspaper company for them out of our profits.

Out of every two cents, Ba-ba was allowed to keep three-quarters of a cent as his profit, so my share of the take was about one dollar and a half a week. That was big money in those days for a nine-year-old kid.

Three years later, Ba-ba decided to work on the tobacco farms in Windsor, Connecticut. He sold his entire route to me. That meant I needed a bike because the route had grown to eighty customers.

Ba-ba tagged along with me when I bought the bike. I still had it six years later when I entered the service and it was waiting for me when I got out. We went to the Carlisle Hardware Store on North Main Street and sat on a few of the bikes there, all with big, fat balloon tires, New Departure brakes, and wide handle bars just like the motorcycles.

"I see you're back, Mr. Zebrowski," the salesman, Mr. LaRusso, said. "That red, white, and blue one is still here."

I walked over to it. It was a beauty.

"This is the one I like, Mr. LaRusso," I said.

"How do you plan to pay for this, Mr. Zebrowski?"

"H-h-he's got a newspaper route," Ba-ba chimed in.

"Mr. Zebrowski can speak for himself," Mr. LaRusso said.

"G-g-go piss up a tree," Ba-ba said.

"You, young man," Mr. LaRusso said angrily, "can wait outside if you think you're so smart."

Ba-ba went outside and waited without saying another word. Thank God he knew when to shut up once he said too much.

"That bicycle is thirty-nine dollars and fifty cents, Mr. Zebrowski. You will need five dollars down and you will have to come to the store every week and pay one dollar on account until the entire amount is paid for. If you miss a payment, we'll be forced to take the bicycle back and you will forfeit everything you paid. Do you agree with those terms?"

I pulled out five dollars in change that I had saved over the three years that I had been in the newspaper business and drove the bicycle home with Ba-ba on the bar.

"I don't know why people get so mad when I tell them to go piss up a tree," Ba-ba said on the way home.

"They probably don't want anybody to think that they've tried anything that foolish, now that they're grown up," I said. "You know once you're grown up you're supposed to act dignified."

The bike rode like a dream.

There was one customer that Ba-ba hated to turn over to me and that was Mrs. Angie Martinelli. She was twenty-four and already divorced and was always taking a bath when Ba-ba went there on Saturdays to collect for the paper.

"Come in, Camille," she would sing out from the bathroom, the door partially open. "The money's on the table, Camille, fifteen cents. And there's a glass of milk and some cookies for you, too."

Ba-ba often told me that when he heard those words, he would mutter under his breath, "I'd rather have those cookies you're washing, Mrs. Martinelli."

She would step out of the tub and towel herself dry while Ba-ba would be choking on the cookies and milk as he watched her through the open door. Apparently she enjoyed having him peep, and of course, Ba-ba always enjoyed peeping. It never went past the peeping stage, even though he said confidently that he could have handled the situation if it had done so.

Soon after I took over the route, Mrs. Martinelli found a new boyfriend and she no longer had to take her baths during Saturday collections, but the few good peeps I got were certainly worth it. If she had only realized she could have gotten her newspapers delivered free for the rest of her life.

Every morning before school started we'd cross over the railroad tracks and go to Ba-ba's house. He taught us a new method for keeping our hair in place even in winds over one hundred miles an hour. It was very simple and I wondered why I hadn't thought of it myself. First, you wet your hair, then soap up your hands, and finally, rub the soapy froth well into your hair. After combing your hair and letting it dry, the result was like a steel helmet. Nothing could penetrate it. All of us used this method. We have school pictures to prove it. It was absolutely dependable, except when it rained.

We had very little wood or coal to burn in the one stove that was in the kitchen in our house. There was no central heating. Money was scarce. Ba-ba and I would go down the tracks with pails and pick up the coal that fell off the trains. The coal was especially plentiful around the curves. When we ran out of coal, Ba-ba thought that corn cobs would burn well in the stove. There was a feed mill at the end of Prospect Street that always had a big supply. The foreman was very happy to give them to us because it saved him money. Previously, he had to hire someone to haul them to the dump.

Ba-ba was right. The corn cobs burned well but didn't last long. Because we had a never-ending supply, thanks to Ba-ba's good thinking, we didn't care.

Times were so bad that both the water and the electricity were shut off in my house at the same time. We hadn't paid the rent for a long time and the landlord hoped this would force us to move. But there was no other place to go so we stayed right there.

Ba-ba and I lugged pails of water from his house to mine until we were blue in the face. Then we relaxed by eating wild blackberries that grew in the fields behind my house.

One day Ba-ba was late in coming down to the river in back of his house where we were fishing for bluegills and redgills using bread dough for bait. The fish were in a feeding frenzy and we were hauling them in.

"D-d-drop your rods, boys," Ba-ba said when he finally got there. "I hit the jackpot this morning and the banana splits are on me."

We walked up South Street to Tatoian's Ice Cream Parlor and Candy Store that was located on Pearl street. The whole gang of us ordered large banana splits. Donald Robinson, Chichi Padrevita, Arthur Rossi, and my brother, Joe, each had two. When Ba-ba told Mr. Tatoian to put it all on one bill, the old man gave him a suspicious look.

"And who, if I may be so bold as to ask, is the rich man's son who is going to pay for all this?" he asked, his arms folded across his chest.

We all pointed to Ba-ba.

"T-t-that's right," Ba-ba said. "And bring me a pack of Lucky Strikes while you're at it, old man."

He took out a wad of bills from his pocket and Mr. Tatoian was quickly convinced.

"Be satisfied with the ice cream, young man," Mr. Tatoian said. "You're too young to smoke."

We gorged ourselves on the banana splits and Ba-ba paid the check with the royal bearing of King George VI conferring knighthood on some of his subjects. We then went down Pearl Street to the Five and Ten Cent Store and bought some tennis balls, tooth brushes, tooth paste, and a variety of other things. Ba-ba again pulled out his roll of bills. Licking his thumb, he peeled off a few and paid the lady who had been watching us like a hawk, worried that we might stuff our pockets with her merchandise. Ba-ba blew around twenty bucks in about two hours. We all offered him our profuse thanks for his exceptional generosity.

"That's all right, boys," he said, puffing on one of the cigarettes he had managed to buy at another store down the block. "I know you'll do the same when you come into some money like I did."

The next day when we saw Ba-ba, he had two black eyes and a swollen nose. He confessed to us that he had temporarily "borrowed" the money from his older brother, Yvon.

When Yvon came home from work and found that the money

had disappeared, he went stark raving mad and beat the shit out of Ba-ba.

"H-h-he didn't even ask around to see who was guilty," Ba-ba said. "H-h-he just beat the hell out of me, guessing that I was the one. And the worst part of it was, he knew all along that I'd pay it back. W-w-what do you think of that for a royal bastard of a brother?"

He rubbed his swollen nose gently.

"J-J-Jesus, we had a good time, though, didn't we? It was almost worth it. But I'll tell you something. I'll never borrow any money from my brother again. You can bet your life on it. He's really a sore lender."

On Sundays, the big motor launches would cruise down the river from Springfield, Massachusetts. The Windsor Locks Canal was open at that time. The canal bypassed the Enfield Falls so the boats had a clear passage all the way to Long Island Sound. Many of the boats were filled with people so drunk they could barely move. We could hear them from the shore, laughing, hollering, giggling, and puking. Even though we were in the middle of a severe depression, it appeared there were still many people with plenty of money to burn.

Some of the boats, drifting with the current, came dangerously close to the falls. We never did see any of the boats go over, but there were a lot of close calls.

The same Sunday that Ba-ba was thrashed within an inch of his life, one launch came closer to the falls than any of the others. Ba-ba and I sat watching it from the shore, drifting lazily past us with the current. There were no signs of life aboard.

"Ba-ba," I yelled out. "We might be in luck. That boat looks abandoned."

"Ba-ba-balls, Zeb," he answered. "They're just plain drunk."

He sat there unconcerned, skinning a branch for a new fishing pole. The boat kept drifting down the river, picking up speed, it seemed, as it got closer and closer to the falls.

Ba-ba finally looked up. He threw down his pole and jumped up.

"You're right, Zeb. I didn't think they were that close. That boat's going over the falls if we don't get out there fast."

We broke the chain on one of the aluminum rowboats moored to the trees along the river and, using boards we found along the bank, paddled furiously down the river, finally catching up with the drifting motor launch.

Ba-ba hopped inside while I held the two boats together.

"Get the anchor, Ba-ba," I yelled out. "Quick, the current is getting faster."

But Ba-ba already had the anchor. He dropped it over the side and it snagged against some rocks on the bottom and the boat steadied. We were only a few hundred yards from the falls and the current was dangerously swift. The roar of the falls drowned out our voices. I kept thinking of the Moriarty brothers who had drowned when they had gone over the falls in a rowboat just like the one we had taken.

Ba-ba disappeared inside the cabin of the launch. He seemed to be gone a long time.

"Ba," I yelled as loud as I could. "What the hell are you doing in there?"

A red flare shot out of the cabin with a frightening swoosh and I saw Ba-ba come jumping out like a big jack rabbit. With one bound he leaped back into the rowboat and started to paddle for all his life, even before I let go of the launch.

"T-t-that son-of-a-bitch is crazy," he said, ramming the launch with his board to shove off. "Paddle, Zeb, paddle, or we're going to get a flare up our asses. That bastard is trying to kill me."

We paddled frantically.

I looked back over my shoulder to see what threw Ba-ba into this frenzy. I saw a bare-assed guy staggering around the deck with a flare gun in his right hand.

"He's going to shoot again, Zeb, for Christ sakes keep paddling," Ba-ba yelled out, still in a panic.

The second flare shot over our heads and sizzled in the water ahead of us.

"What the hell is he so mad about, Ba-ba? We saved his rotten, lousy ass."

"Keep paddling, Zeb. Those falls are awfully close and that nut with the flare gun is as mad as a crazy bull."

We finally got to shore, our arms ready to fall off.

"T-t-that crazy, drunken bastard nearly shot off my ba-ba-balls," Ba-ba said.

"Why was he so mad?"

"W-w-well," Ba-ba said, "there they were, this broad and her boyfriend, who was old enough to be her father. They were both drunk to the gills, smelling of vomit and both bare-assed. She had two of the biggest baboozles you ever saw in your whole life, Zeb. Honest, they were so big when she was lying on her back, one was pointing to the Suffield Rocks and the other to the Well on the Enfield side. They were even bigger than my sister Liza's. That bare-assed guy you saw staggering around on deck was lying half on top of her. When I saw those big baboozles, I nearly went crazy myself. I thought they were both out like a light so I reached over and gave her tit a little twit. The old guy must have been watching me, playing possum, you know, because before I knew what was happening, he jumped up like a wild animal. I couldn't even understand what he was saying. He was just howling. Maybe it wasn't even English. He grabbed the flare gun and lets one go right at my ba-ba-balls. I could feel the heat as it passed between my legs. If I didn't jump just at the right time, you'd be taking me to the hospital right now and I'd be singing soprano. That was a close one, Zeb, let me tell you. My career as the greatest pisser in the world would have ended right then and there."

Ba-ba sat on an old tree stump on the shore holding onto his crotch as though he was still under fire.

"You know, Zeb, touching that big tit was worth it, though."

"Yeah, worth it for you, Ba-ba," I said. "You get all the action and all I get is the story. If that flare had hit me in the ass while we were paddling for our lives, I'd never have forgiven you. Why do all the interesting things always seem to happen to you?"

"I guess I'm just a lucky guy, Zeb," Ba-ba said, laughing.

"Did you ever see Liza like that, Ba-ba, like that dame on the boat?"

Ba-ba knew I had a crush on his older sister.

"W-w-well, you know I sort of had the habit of trying to barge in on Liza when s-s-she went to her room or took a bath. B-b-but she always locked the door, d-d-dammit. This one time, though, she either forgot or she really wanted me to see her bare, because all of a sudden, there I was face to face with her a-a-ass, the nicest looking thing in this whole wide world."

"Jehoosis," I said. "I would have given anything in the world to have been there with you."

I scaled a flat stone across the water and counted out loud as it made ten hops.

"I don't think you could have stood it, Zeb. All the blood would have rushed out of your brain into your dick and you would have collapsed in shock. Anyway, she let out a squeal that sounded like I had stepped on her cat and I just stood there frozen."

"You mean Liza just stood there, too, and let you look?"

"L-l-like hell she did. She leaned over and slugged me right on the nose. Blood shot out all over the place. Then she gave me a big push and I landed half-way across the hall on my b-b-back and the door slammed shut. She could have busted all my bones and it would have been worth it. R-r-right then and there, I made up my mind that when I got married, my wife would have to have an a-a-ass as big and round as Liza's, and two big beautiful baboozles just like hers."

Ba-ba sat there thinking for awhile, savoring that lovely image in his brain. Even then we all recognized that he had a deep understanding of the fundamental things in life.

One afternoon, after our usual drinking and pissing contests, we stood on the lip of the Well, the red shale bright in the sunlight.

"We can't swim in that water today, Zeb," Ba-ba said, pointing down at the river.

There was a grand and stately parade of turds floating majestically past us, little islands suspended on the surface of the river in a never-ending stream. Occasionally, a pale white condom would glide by silently, a ghostly orgasm congealed in time. The water was green and blue and red at different times from the dyes dumped into it by the Bigelow Sanford Carpet Company, a couple of miles upstream.

"A-a-a lot of white fish floating by, Zeb," Ba-ba said, pointing to the condoms sadly. "A lot of guys have been awfully busy in Thompsonville."

"Yeah, and here we are doing nothing. Why don't we go swimming at the Suffield Rocks?"

Because of the currents, the water at the Suffield Rocks, which was just across the river above the dam, was usually clear, even though the river itself was heavily polluted.

The Public Health Department offered free tetanus toxoid shots every year because it was a well-known fact that everybody swam in the river.

We slipped a link, as we usually did hundreds of times before, on one of the boats chained along the river in back of Ba-ba's house and paddled across with the usual old boards.

"Now that's more like it, Zeb," Ba-ba said, squinting against the reflection of the sun as he looked at the water closely to see the bottom.

It was clear as we had expected and the rocky bottom, with patches of sand and strewn boulders, was clearly visible. We stripped and jumped in, splashing and yelling. We swam out about fifty feet, Ba-ba only a short distance from me, when I suddenly got a severe cramp in my right leg and went under. I panicked, swallowed some water the wrong way, coughed, and swallowed some more water. My chest felt like it was going to burst. I came up for a moment and tried to yell to Ba-ba, but all I got for my effort was another mouthful of water. I went under again, feeling this was really the end. My chest was ready to explode and the last thing I remembered was what an awful shame it was going to be to miss out on all those girls with big round bottoms and large baboozles like Ba-ba's sister, Liza.

The next thing I knew, I was on the shore and Ba-ba was working over me furiously, pumping my chest, slapping my face, swearing, grunting, and saying rapidly, "Don't die now, Zeb, don't die now. Please God, don't let him die, please, please, please."

As I came to, I thought Ba-ba was reciting his rosary beads. There was no stuttering, but the spit was flying, peppering my face like a machine gun. I think that's what really got me breathing again.

"OK, OK, OK," I said, finally. "I promise not to die, Ba-ba."

I was coughing, snorting, and spitting and my eyes were blinking a thousand blinks a minute against his spitballs.

Ba-ba let out a long sigh, his whole body shuddering. He threw himself on the shore along side of me and closed his eyes against the sun.

"J-J-Jesus, you scared me, Zeb. You were bluer than a blueberry."

"I'd be floating down the river over the dam like all those turds and white fish if you hadn't pulled me out of the water, Ba," I said, still gasping, lying limp and totally exhausted.

Ba didn't answer. His eyes were closed and he was breathing rapidly. We both went to sleep on the shore, our bodies still twitching and shuddering intermittently.

Once a year, Ba-ba would have his throat blessed at St. Patrick's Church, a grand old brown-stone building on the corner of Pearl and High. He would then have tonsillitis off and on all the rest of the winter.

"Ba-ba, did you ever think that maybe having your throat blessed was the cause of all your sore throats?"

"Ba-ba-balls, Zeb. You're all wet. If I didn't get my t-t-throat blessed every year, I'd be a lot sicker. It's like being vaccinated or getting a tetanus shot. What made you say that?"

"Well, I never get my throat blessed and I don't get sore throats, Ba-ba. And furthermore, if I was going to think like the devil, where would I hang out to do the most evil? Around all the churches, of course, because that's where all the religious people go. And besides, most of the people will be coughing and sneezing now that it's getting cold, and you'll probably catch something just being there."

"I never thought of that," Ba-ba said. "But I'm still going to get my throat blessed and you're going to go with me."

"Nah, I can't go with you, Ba-ba. Anyway, if I was going to have a part of my body blessed, I'd rather have my crotch blessed instead of my throat."

"I-I-I never heard of any crotches being blessed in the Catholic churches but that sounds like a good idea. I'll have to ask Father Graham about that. But you're coming with me this time. It's very simple, you know. Father Graham will hold up two crossed candles under your throat, mutter a few words that nobody understands, and that's it. It's all over in a flash and you don't have to wear a camphor bag around your neck all winter."

"That sounds like a lot of bullshit to me, Ba-ba. How can that kind of hocus-pocus have any effect on the germs in your mouth?"

"God is supposed to protect you against those germs, Zeb."

"Who created those germs in the first place, Ba-ba?"

"God, I suppose."

"Well, what is He playing, some kind of silly game? He creates germs to make us sick, and then we have to go to church and go through some kind of mumbo-jumbo to protect us from the germs He created. That sounds kind of stupid, don't you think?"

"I never thought of it that way before, Zeb."

"Anyway," I said. "I'd rather take sulfa tablets."

"Y-y-yeah, I guess sulfa is good, but it costs money. Getting your throat blessed is free. Maybe a priest is like a doctor for poor people."

"Anyway, I'm an atheist, Ba," I said.

"An-an-an atheist?" Ba looked surprised. "Since when?"

"Since last Thursday, that's when."

"What happened last Thursday, Zeb?"

"I was reading a book describing atheism and I suddenly realized what I really believe."

"I-I-I only read the catechism, Zeb, and not much of that, either. You mean you don't believe in G-G-God?"

"Nah, I don't go for that bullshit, Ba. But I don't mind if other people do."

"J-J-Jesus, Zeb, I hope you don't get struck by lightning."

"I never have yet, Ba, and I don't think I ever will. Just remember, the God you believe in is supposed to have given everybody free will. So I'm thinking like I want to think and that shouldn't make anybody mad, especially a God or any truly religious person."

"W-w-well, it won't hurt you to have your throat blessed no matter what way you think," Ba-ba said, "so you have to come."

"I'm telling you, Ba, atheists don't have their throats blessed."

"How did you learn to become an atheist, Zeb? Do you have a catechism like we do?"

"Nah, there's no catechism but I think that's a good idea. I guess I learned from my oldest brother, Stan, who is like a father to me. He's twenty years older than I am. He and I always talk about deep things, you know, like the meaning of life."

"Talking about girls is a lot more fun. W-w-where did he learn about being an atheist?"

"Up at college, I guess. At Dartmouth. That's where I plan to go

127

when I finish high school."

"Do they teach that at Dartmouth?"

"I don't think so. I think they teach you everything you're supposed to know about any subject and then you can decide for yourself. They don't force you to think any special way."

"W-w-well anyway, Zeb, you can be the first atheist to have his throat blessed in Thompsonville, Connecticut. You have to come."

"I can't, Ba-ba."

"You mean you're not broad-minded, Zeb?"

"Of course, I'm broad-minded, Ba. I always told you that, didn't I?"

"N-n-no you're not, Zeb. Not if you don't have your throat blessed. Anyway, I'll sneak you in through the basement, s-s-so no other atheists will see you."

Ba-ba was very persuasive and very determined.

"All right, I'll try it only because you want me to, Ba," I finally said.

"You'll see it works, Zeb. You'll see."

The church was dark and chilly and there was a long line of people. A light rain was falling.

"I'm only doing this for you, Ba. You know that."

"You won't be sorry, Zeb. I promise you."

We finally had our turn at the altar. Father Graham spoke under his breath in a flat monotone as he went rapidly from person to person. It was over before I could blink my eyes.

Outside the church Ba looked at me as if he expected some miraculous transformation.

"Now Zeb, tell me honestly, don't you feel better?"

"Not yet, Ba," I said, swallowing and feeling my throat. "I felt good before and I feel good now."

"This is going to be the best winter you ever had, Zeb. I promise you. You might even turn Catholic and then the two of us can go to Hell together."

The next morning I woke up with a hot fire in my throat and I was burning up with fever. My mother gave me sips of hot, melted butter that she salted heavily, the poor people's substitute for sulfa. I didn't see Ba-ba for three days. When I finally did see him, I poked a finger in his chest.

"Ba-ba," I said, "you are full of shit."

"N-n-now what did I do, Zeb?"

"You sweet-talked me into getting my throat blessed and then I had the worst sore throat of my life."

"S-s-so did I, Zeb. It must have been the rain or Father Graham forgot to say some of the words. Besides, it was chilly that night. Or maybe the devil was doing his dirty work at the church just like you said. Anyway, you would have been much worse without the blessing."

"I don't believe that, Ba. But I can see you are fast with excuses."

"Father Graham says the ways of the Lord are mysterious, Zeb," Ba-ba said, feeling his neck.

"You can say that again, Ba. Maybe if I get my throat blessed again next year, God might give me cancer. And I suppose I'll have to accept that as His overall plan."

When Ba-ba turned sixteen, he got a job at the big A&P Store on Pearl Street, just down the street from where I worked in the morning in a little corner variety store run by Pete Kapinos. Pete had a wooden leg and couldn't get around too well, so I picked up the bundle of Springfield Union newspapers at the train station every morning at four-thirty. I opened up the store for all the guys who were going to work hung over from the night before in dire need of an emergency dose of Alka Seltzer and a fresh pack of butts.

When I turned sixteen, I sold my newspaper route and got a job at the A&P, too. I had to quit my job with Pete Kapinos, even though I felt sorry about his wooden leg. All my friends were already working at the A&P. School ended at twelve-thirty and we started work at one o'clock. There was no lunch. The store closed at six, but it was about seven-thirty before the last customer left. We were paid only to six, which caused a lot of griping and snitching of candy and gum. On Saturdays, we worked from eight in the morning to ten-thirty at night. The store closed at nine, but again we had to work until the last customer left, even though our pay stopped at nine o'clock. Tuesdays and Thursdays were freight nights. When all the customers were finally gone, we unloaded all the big trailer trucks and the aisles were completely cluttered with boxes of all kinds of canned goods. We usually got out of work around two in the morning. We got on our bikes, which we didn't keep chained because nobody ever stole them, and rode home. It was back to school at eight. There were no buses, but it was only a two-mile walk.

We were paid thirty-five cents a hour. For one week's work of fifty-four hours, we received a grand total of eighteen dollars and ninety cents minus deductions.

After I had worked there for about three months, Ba-ba and all the rest of the guys were grumbling about the long hours and the small amount of money we earned. We had a few discussions and finally decided to ask for forty cents an hour or quit en masse. I was delegated as spokesman even though I was the newest employee and the youngest one there.

On a Tuesday night at ten o'clock, with all the aisles filled with boxes, I went up to Mr. O'Brien, the manager, a big fat man weighing over three hundred pounds. He used to be one of my good newspaper customers who paid regularly fifteen cents every Saturday.

"Mr. O'Brien," I said, my knees shaking.

"What's the problem, Zeb?" he asked, turning his huge body to look at me. Because of his immense weight, he always seemed to be sweating and breathing hard, like Mr. Pickwick in one of Charles Dickens' books.

"All the boys have been talking about how little money we make here and the long hours," I said.

"Any other complaints?" Mr. O'Brien asked, rather pleasantly.

"We don't like the fact that we don't get paid for the hour and a half after the store closes in the evenings," I added.

"And...," Mr. O'Brien said. He didn't act upset, but he didn't look like he was going to make it easy for me, either.

"Well, we thought that we'd like to get per hour what they get over at Grant's across the street."

"And what's that, Zeb?" Mr. O'Brien asked.

"Forty cents an hour," I said.

"Well, why don't you?" Mr. O'Brien asked, taking out a handkerchief and wiping his brow.

I knew that I wasn't the cause of his sweating. He was taking the discussion calmly.

"Why don't I what?" I asked.

"Why don't you go across the street and get forty cents an hour?" Mr. O'Brien said.

He acted as if he was discussing the weather instead of the financial lives of all his young workers. I began to realize that the art of negotiation was not easily learned and that it required experience I didn't have at the age of sixteen.

I began to fumble for words, not having planned on a lengthy debate. Mr. O'Brien, seeing my hesitation and sensing an opening, thrust his A&P sword right through my heart.

"You see that door there, Zeb?" He pointed to the rear of the store. "That's the way out."

He turned away and continued on with his work as if nothing had happened.

"Can't we discuss this, Mr. O'Brien?" I asked, feeling a little sick to my stomach.

"We already have, Zeb," he said without turning around. "You know where the door is, but if you want to work, it's there on the floor waiting for you."

I stood there for awhile, not knowing what to say next. I saw Ba-ba looking at me. I shrugged my shoulders, pointing my right thumb down, and started toward the rear of the store. As I crossed every aisle, I waved at all the guys to follow me. I was afraid to look back to see if they were coming. It was too damned quiet in the store. When I got to the rear door, I turned around. All the guys were there behind me, one hundred percent.

"Now wait a minute, fellas," Mr. O'Brien yelled out.

He had finally turned around and saw the silent parade marching in step to the rear door. Now he knew we weren't talking about the weather.

"I didn't know it was the whole damn bunch of you," he said, a note of panic in his voice as he looked at all the merchandise on the floor of all the aisles. "Go back to work. You've got your forty cents."

Ba-ba smiled at me, and gave me the thumbs-up sign. I gave it back to him. It was a great feeling for all of us.

"Y-y-you did it, Zeb. You did it. I knew you'd come through."

That Saturday we were all fired. Mr. O'Brien brought in a whole new team of high-school kids bussed in from Springfield, Massachusetts.

About two weeks later, Ba-ba and I were riding by the store on our bicycles when we saw Mr. O'Brien through the plate glass window waving at us to come in.

"You both can have your old jobs back at forty cents an hour, boys," Mr. O'Brien said. "I know that you're good workers and deserve the raise. What do you say?"

I looked at Ba and he pointed his finger at me to go ahead with the answer. I knew that he would go along with whatever I said.

"Are you going to take everybody back at the same rate, Mr. O'Brien?" I asked.

"No, I can't do that, boys," Mr. O'Brien said. "Just you two."

We turned him down politely, thanked him for giving us the offer and left.

By then, war had been declared against Japan and Germany and there was plenty of work everywhere. All of us applied to the Bigelow Sanford Carpet Company, where they had converted their looms to weaving blankets for the military services. We were hired on the spot. Our work schedule was four hours a day during school days, eight hours on Saturday, for which we were paid time-and-a-half, and eight hours on Sunday, which was double time, all at sixty-six and one-half cents an hour. That meant we were paid forty-eight hours for thirty-six hours of work and took home a gross pay of thirty-one dollars and ninety-two cents. We were suddenly in the money.

Within two weeks at the Bigelow, Ba-ba was already diddling one of the lady inspectors, a married woman whose husband was in the service. She had big baboozles and a big round behind. She was built like his sister Liza and his spitball mouth did not appear to be an obstacle to his love-making. Apparently he didn't talk much when he was with her. He just got right down to work. We all expressed our admiration for his leadership qualities and hoped we could be as successful as he was.

About one month after we had been working at Bigelow, Ba-ba

came to me with a plan to improve our working conditions.

"Remember what happened the last time we tried to do that, Ba," I said, waving my index finger at him.

"Y-y-yeah, I know, but this is different," he said.

Our work required us to roll up the unfinished blanket rolls after the ladies inspected and repaired any defects. These were large rolls and required two men to roll them up evenly and hoist them up on a four-wheel dolly. When we had a total of twelve rolls, four rolls to a dolly, we pushed the loaded dollies across a paved area to the dye house where the blankets were washed, dyed, and napped. During a four-hour stint, we were required to load and deliver forty-eight rolls, besides making sure all the lady inspectors had new rolls of blankets to inspect and repair.

"We can do the whole damn work load in two hours," Ba-ba said, after analyzing the situation, "especially if we work our asses off."

"Yes, I think we can," I said.

"Then we can screw off for the other two hours," Ba-ba said, confidently.

"We'll be running a risk, you know, of being caught."

"Not much," Ba-ba said. "The ladies will warn us if anybody's coming."

That was just like Ba-ba. He thought of everything.

The plan worked beautifully. The lady inspectors were happy, especially the one Ba was diddling. The dye house foreman was happy, and so were we.

We'd play football or baseball during the second two hours in between some old unused carpet looms. Baseball was especially demanding because the baseball we used was a tightly rolled up paper bag tied with a string, about three by four inches. Our bat was a four-foot broom stick handle. You'd have to have a good eye and excellent timing to get a hit. Ba-ba , as usual, was our home run hitter. One day Ba-ba and I collided. Dr. Dignam, the factory physician, inserted four sutures to close the wound over my left eye. I told him I had accidentally slipped and fallen on one of the hand trucks.

After horsing around for an hour or so, we would all take a nap on some of the blanket rolls we saved for that purpose. Occasionally, the cockroaches bothered us, especially if they crawled on our faces, but they rarely woke us up.

One day while we were all sleeping, we were suddenly awakened by a very loud voice.

"I knew I'd catch you young bastards sooner or later. Now get out, get out, you're all fired. Get off the grounds immediately."

Mr. John Fuge, the superintendent of the Axminster Department, was standing over us with his hands on his hips, yelling at us as loud as he could, his face as red as the yarn in an Axminster carpet. He was a skinny little fart with a big booming voice.

"Out you go and I never want to see any of you ever again. But before you go, we're all going over to the dye house to talk to the foreman there just to see how much you boys succeeded in slowing down the war effort."

We marched behind him, a sad brigade.

Fortunately, the foreman of the dye house, Joe Scalucci, liked us.

"These kids are the greatest, Mr. Fuge," he said, recognizing immediately that we were in some kind of trouble. "Just look at the dye house. We're loaded to the rafters. We don't have an inch of room left. And these kids will do anything for me. I only wish some of my older workers were as good as these kids."

Mr. Fuge looked disappointed.

Off we marched to the lady inspectors.

"The boys are just simply wonderful. They are right here to help us all the time, and they never complain no matter how many things we ask them to do. They even pile the work on us too much."

Mr. Fuge turned to us, his face still very angry.

"I don't care what these ladies say on your behalf or what Mr. Scalucci says," Mr. Fuge yelled above the noise of the looms. "You're still fired. Now get out."

We got out of there fast. As we walked through the main gate, I looked over at Ba-ba.

"You and your great plan, Ba-ba," I said.

"I think somebody squealed on us," Ba-ba said. "We're getting a reputation fast. Fired from the A&P, and now the Bigelow. Pretty soon we'll have to go out of town to get a job, or just join the army."

That night Ba-ba and I went to see my second oldest brother,

Walt, who was now the assistant superintendent of the Axminster Department, having started there as a trucker at the age of fourteen when we first moved to Thompsonville from Massachusetts in 1929. Twenty-five years later, he became the superintendant of the entire mill.

"That was a stupid thing to do," Walt said, frowning. "I expected more from you two."

Ba-ba kept his mouth shut for once, leaving it up to me to put my foot in my mouth, which I did immediately.

"We didn't expect to get caught," I said.

"Now I'm sure you know I didn't mean about getting caught," Walt said, his anger clearly visible. "I meant about sleeping on the job. You're not being paid good money to sleep. That was dumb and inexcusable."

He was very upset because we had let him down. He made us promise to work at a reasonable pace and to do the work evenly throughout the entire four hours. There was to be no more baseball, football, or sleeping on the job.

"Report to work tomorrow as usual and I'll try to fix it up with Mr. Fuge," he added, clucking his tongue in disgust.

We notified all the other guys who were fired with us. The next day at two o'clock in the afternoon there was Mr. Fuge, standing at the entrance to the Axminster building waiting for us, a terrible storm brewing on his face.

"I should have my head examined, but you young bastards have one more chance to prove you're not worthless bums. In another year or so, all of you will probably be in the service getting your asses blown to hell and gone, over there fighting the Germans and the Japs, anyway."

Six months later, Ba-ba quit high school and enlisted in the army. One year after that, I did the same thing.

****

I didn't see him again until he stepped out of that Sherman tank at Braunau, Austria, on May 1, 1945, standing there tall and smiling in the sun, seven days before the war officially ended.

Morelli came over to me and put his hand on my shoulder while

I held Ba-ba in my arms.

"He's dead, Zeb," he said quietly.

I sat there crying.

Chapter 13

The Pine Forest

"**Z**eb," Morelli called softly. He was shaking me gently by the shoulder.

"What's up?" I said, turning over quickly, startled.

"You're moaning in your sleep and keeping everybody awake," Morelli said. "What's the matter?"

"I was dreaming that I was back in the Pine Forest again," I said. "I was surrounded by all those poor dying bastards lying in that muck and I dreamt that I was dying with them. It was horrible."

"I heard you moaning, Zeb," Morelli said, "and I was still half-asleep and I was dreaming that you and I were there together, too."

"Have you got watch tonight?" I said.

"No. Go back to sleep. It's only two o'clock."

****

It was May 4, 1945, and our platoon had just gone through Lambach, Austria. As usual, white sheets were billowing out of the windows and there were no Germans soldiers in sight. Since leaving Braunau, the village where Adolf Hitler was born, there had been no real resistance and the Germans were surrendering in droves. They were coming out of the woods, the houses, the barns, and the cellars, with their hands clasped on top of their heads, their weapons discarded. We just pointed them down the road where the front line infantry battalions would eventually pick them up.

It was a bright spring day and we were traveling slowly on a narrow dirt road. The two months we had been in combat taught us to be on guard at all times and that day was no exception. Even though we felt the war was finally coming to an end, we knew there were still many Germans who were determined to fight to the bitter end, especially the Waffen SS units. The dust the jeeps kicked up was dense and stifling. I kept my left hand over my mouth and nose, holding my M1 with my right. That was when we entered a thick forest of pines.

> *The Lord is my shepherd, I*
> *shall not want.*
> *He maketh me to lie down in green pastures:*
> *He leadeth me beside the still waters.*
> *He restoreth my soul.*
> *He leadeth me in the paths of righteousness*
> *for His name's sake.*

At first, there was the fresh clean smell of pine that filled the air. And then another scent, initially difficult to recognize but definitely repugnant, drifted through the air like a noxious gas. It gradually became stronger as we penetrated deeper into the woods. The sunlight was quickly obliterated and the sudden change made it difficult to see. It was like entering a different world that had a foul and loathsome landscape.

Off to the left, a few yards from the road, we saw what looked like a pile of old, dirty, discarded clothes. As we came closer, we were shocked to see the pile move. A face slowly turned towards us. It was smeared with grime, the skin taut against the bones of the face, emaciated, the mouth open and mumbling unintelligible sounds, the teeth rotten stumps, the eyes like empty black holes looking at us, but not understanding the images transmitted to its numbed brain. Vermin were crawling over encrusted ulcerations. One arm rose from the muck in which he lay, extended towards us in an excruciating plea for help. Was this a human being, I thought shuddering, or was this some pathetic starving, filthy, injured animal that had escaped from a monstrous and insane keeper?

As our eyes adjusted to the light, we saw others gradually take form in the darkness of the woods, rising from the decaying ground like corpses from a graveyard, first a few, then hundreds. For every one we saw rising in a horrible, irregular, agonizing succession of motions, we knew instantly that there were hundreds of others who would never rise again. The stench was so over-powering it made us gag. It was a mighty, moving swell of human excrement, urine, and rotting flesh mixed with the acrid smell of German tobacco smoke. It hung about us like a poisonous gas, suffocating, sticky, pungent, clinging to our clothes, our hair, and our nostrils until we thought we would never breathe good, clean, fresh air again.

I kept seeing them slowly dragging towards us, just as in my dreams that night, their movements jerky and unsteady, hesitant, awkward, their eyes blank and devoid of emotion, not yet aware they were now free men.

They gestured feebly with their fingers pointing to their mouths, "wasser, brot, essen," fragile words cast upon the damp forest air like dead leaves, whispered softly and barely audible so that we were not sure that we heard them at all.

> *Yea, though I walk through the*
> *valley of the shadow of death,*
> *I will fear no evil;*
> *for Thou art with me;*
> *Thy rod and Thy staff,*
> *they comfort me.*

****

I couldn't sleep after Morelli woke me up. I heard him tossing and turning. I shut my eyes tight, because I knew I could no longer tolerate seeing those dying people, my nose could no longer endure the stench of their dying, and my ears could no longer bear to hear the mournful dirge of their incomprehensible babble. It seemed we were doomed to relive that excursion into Hell forever, I thought, and we would be lucky if it didn't drive us all mad.

****

Thou preparest a table before me
in the presence of mine enemies;
Thou annointest my head with oil;
my cup runneth over.

We came to a railroad crossing with hundreds of boxcars on a long siding. In front of each was a huge pile of corpses, ready to be hauled off to some mass grave. We had arrived too soon for the Waffen SS to conceal this horror.

Eventually we couldn't go any farther, being surrounded by this ever-increasing tide of death. We unloaded all our K rations and water and those miserable, tortured souls reached out to touch us as if unable to comprehend that we were real and not mere figments of their imagination. Hands stretched out, tremulous, gaunt, like blackened claws, grimy, crawling with insects, covered with scabrous sores; and as they reached out, we instinctively pulled back, unable to control our nausea and dread.

As some of them came over, using their last bits of strength, they gasped and died in front of us, a last silent scream on their swollen, pustular lips, their bodies dropping right at our feet, once again becoming part of the rotting muck there.

Surely, goodness and mercy shall follow me
all the days of my life;
And I shall dwell in the house
of the Lord
forever.

****

Later, we found out that we had gone through Gunskirchen Lager, a concentration camp for eighteen thousand prisoners of the Nazis, composed mostly of Hungarian Jews, Russians, Poles, Frenchmen, Yugoslavs, and Czechs. Extreme starvation wasted their features until they all looked alike.

The Waffen SS in charge of the camp had left two days before we arrived, hurriedly burying some of the dead in huge holes. But the number of dead was overwhelming, causing the soldiers to leave before they could hide the horrible evidence of their inhumanity.

The prisoners had had no food or water for five days and before that, they had been given one cube of sugar each and one loaf of bread to be divided among seven individuals.

There were three thousand starving and dying human beings crowded into each of a half-dozen crude log cabins designed to hold three hundred. The dirt floors had degenerated into a foul muck. One twenty-hole latrine served the entire camp. Thousands suffered from dysentery and were forced to stand in line for hours waiting to empty their bowels. Many were shot on the spot when they were unable to control themselves in other areas of the camp. In the buildings, there was so little room they had to sleep on top of one another. When some of them died, the others were too weak to drag their corpses outside, so they continued to lie on their decomposing bodies. There were half-devoured, rotting carcasses of horses scattered around the camp.

Many of the Jews had just recently arrived from Hungary after a long death march without any food or water. In their ranks were physicians, attorneys, chemists, professors, and concert musicians, all reduced to the level of starving animals. They had marched about two hundred miles, wasting away from lack of food. Many died on the way. Others were shot to death as they dared to fall out of line from extreme exhaustion.

****

As we left the Pine Forest, we all felt as though we had suddenly escaped from a prison of the damned. But we knew in our hearts that total escape was truly impossible. During the few hours it took to drive through the Pine Forest, we were changed forever, and the images that were etched into our brains would remain there until the day we died. And if we cried or moaned in our sleep and then suddenly awoke in a cold sweat, we knew we had been back there among the pines, riding again through the darkness of the woods, a silent caravan of ghosts doomed to return forever to view the dead and the dying.

Chapter 14

After the War

As far as our platoon was concerned, the war ended for us with our last mission on May 5, 1945, the day McHugh was killed. We were billeted in a physician's house at the base of that long hill leading out of Steyr. The house was not elaborate but better than average. We were very comfortable there. It was stuccoed and painted a pale tan. There was a pleasant, fenced-in garden area to one side that provided plenty of privacy. For a few days we did nothing but eat, sleep, and drink. Nobody in our platoon was a heavy drinker, but all of us tried out the schnapps in a five gallon jug that one of the men managed to find. To me it was pure firewater, just about equivalent to the Calvados we drank in Normandy.

Thousands of prisoners of war marched past our quarters every day on their way to POW camps set up by the U.S. 3rd Army. Their faces were blank, totally devoid of any visible emotion. Their uniforms were filthy and tattered. They looked exactly like what they were, a completely routed and defeated army.

We assisted in processing thousands of these prisoners in the repatriation program set up in Steyr, providing them with new identification papers and finally delousing them and sending them on their long journey home.

Our house was near a bridge that spanned the Enns River. Before the Russians finally got there on May 9, there was a constant stream of German soldiers and civilians crossing over at that point to escape from them. They just drifted in with all the other POWs. This overwhelming tide of humanity stopped abruptly when the Russian soldiers made their appearance. Every night after that we'd hear rifle and machine gun fire from the Russian side of the river. We became suspicious about the kind of games the Russians were playing. One morning we went down to the river to see for ourselves. There were scattered bodies of German soldiers and civilians lying along the shore, people who had attempted to swim across and apparently were used for target practice by the Russian soldiers. It was a terrible spectacle to see, a shocking display of Russian insensitivity.

For exercise we started to play softball every day in a nearby field. There was a keg of beer on third base and everybody who managed to get that far had to drink a stein of beer before he could advance home. Needless to say, nobody made it home safely, but everybody had a good time.

Two weeks after the war ended, Colonel Wofford threw a huge party for the Russian officers. Naturally, I pulled duty as one of the waiters. General Whitman, the CO of the 71st Division was there, along with many of his staff. All our battalion commanders attended and everybody was friendly and in great spirits, especially after they drank the whole place dry. I didn't come to any conclusion regarding the Russian soldiers as fighters, but as eaters, drinkers, and totally indiscriminate shooters, they were undoubtedly the greatest.

Later on we met many of the younger Russian soldiers. They were about fourteen years old. I am sure they were excellent fighters, because at that age, none of them was mature enough to question the wisdom of any orders given to them by their superior officers.

Two days after this great American-Russian banquet, Kaputt notified us that one of our sergeants in the communications platoon was awarded a battlefield commission. He hadn't done anything spectacular to receive the commission. He just did what was expected of him like all the rest of us. However, on reading the fictional account leading to his commission, anybody would have to conclude he was Audie Murphy, the most decorated soldier in the United States Army. The truth of the matter was a shortage of second lieutenants, because they had the highest loss rate of any of the officers.

The sergeant was very happy with his second lieutenant's bar, as rightly he should have been, even though it would have been embarrassing to read his citation in front of the troops. I'm sure it went over big in his hometown newspapers. Morelli was the first one to salute him as an officer. He gave Morelli a one dollar bill to help him remember that event.

It was also at this time that Kaputt announced that our platoon had been awarded one Silver Star and eight Bronze Stars for our participation in the mission on May 5. He awarded the Silver Star to himself along with one Bronze Star. The sergeant who had been newly commissioned as a second lieutenant wrote up the fictional account of the spectacular deeds Kaputt accomplished that day. We had three sergeants and Kaputt gave each of them a Bronze Star for their heroic action in remaining concealed in the concrete pig pen while McHugh was going through the agony of dying. We also had three corporals and each of them was awarded a Bronze Star. He picked out his favorite pfc for the last medal.

The rest of us were terribly upset about this distribution of medals. All of us had been together for two solid months of combat and this arbitrary recognition of valor and the fictional accounts of battle action made us mad as hell. Most of us felt the platoon should have been cited as a unit. To make things worse, Kaputt had omitted giving McHugh a Bronze Star. This embittered us so much that he finally gave in and awarded the last medal to Mac instead of his favorite pfc. It was sent home to McHugh's mother, a rotten exchange for a son. After all, Mac was the first one to see those 88s that made everybody else scatter. So in truth, he sacrificed his own life to save the rest of the platoon. That was the way we felt about it.

This whole miserable affair with the medals certainly did nothing to make us feel better about our wonderful first lieutenant. In fact, it galvanized our hostility towards him. Of course, we all had our Combat Infantry Badges, awarded to us the first week of combat, which we regarded with great esteem. It seemed to us that everybody who wore this badge was just like a brother. However, our respect for the way the army awarded medals plummeted.

Morelli and I finally got our Bronze Stars in 1990 by a special act of Congress awarding these medals to all infantrymen who had been previously awarded the Combat Infantry Badge. Apparently, the president finally recognized the problem that had occurred in World War II, and by executive order in 1962, made restitution. However, we were never notified of this order until 1990 through our 71st Division Association, thus explaining the long delay in the awards.

It was shortly after this mess that a plot was hatched to get even with Kaputt. The Russian soldiers had told us about the whore house on their side of the river. They said that if we wanted a little sexual diversion at anytime they would let us through the barricade they had set up on their end of the bridge. One of our men asked them if they knew of any women there with gonorrhea. They were surprised to hear that question, because the idea of gonorrhea had never occurred to them. In fact, most of them didn't know what it was. We explained to them that we wanted to pay back our magnificent lieutenant for all the wonderful things he had done for us during the war. They understood very quickly, telling us they had officers like that, too. Most of their officers who behaved like that seemed to die bravely in battle. They liked our idea of getting even and we all downed a few vodkas hoping for a successful conclusion to our plans. Morelli and I got cold feet in the end and decided this was too severe a punishment, even though it was milder than the one the Russians used. The rest of the men, however, were determined to go through with it.

A few days later, the Russians brought over a young, rather frightened, pretty little thing. She was kept in seclusion that night and we threw a party for Kaputt the next day. The young woman was smuggled into his bed in the officers' quarters before the party. We proceeded to get him so drunk he could barely move. We toasted him for the fantastic bravery he exhibited that earned him the Silver Star. We followed up with a toast for his Bronze Star, and for leading us unknowingly through a German mine field without a single casualty, for not taking the offer of three tanks from that tank colonel to go up that road of no return, for being from the great state of Utah, for wearing riding boots to show his individuality, for walking like an old man with painful hemorrhoids, for thinking that President Hoover was a great man, for hating President Roosevelt because he was too liberal, and finally for just being Kaputt. On and on we toasted him through the night. As the schnapps flowed on, the toasts became more and more outrageous, and the laughter roared like cannon fire.

It was about three o'clock in the morning when he was finally brought back to his quarters and dumped into bed beside the young woman, so drunk he could barely talk. She knew what she had to do to earn the money the men had promised to give her.

We learned later that she had performed well, and that Kaputt, after a suitable drying-out period, was also able to do what everybody expected of him. From that day on, for several weeks or so, the young woman was the darling of the officers' quarters, all of them utilizing her services until old "Hooknose", the great healer who gave us the cholera treatment for diarrhea when we were in St. Laurent en Caux, advised them of what she had also given them besides that fleeting moment of sheer rapture. Of course, the Russians got the blame for this short-lived epidemic. And so did our leader, Kaputt. In any event, we didn't shoot the officers, a tribute that some of us felt they richly deserved.

One month after the war ended, the Inspector General of the 20th corps, of which we were a part, made a routine inspection of our division. His conclusion was that it was utterly unbelievable that the 71st Division had been able to move even *one inch* on European soil because of our complete disorganization, let alone be the division that had penetrated farther east than any other outfit in the European Theater of War. We all knew that confusion and uncertainty were always an integral part of any action, but we never realized we were that good. We could only imagine what the other divisions were like. We hoisted a few in honor of that recognition, being the *one-inch* division.

We were in the chow line one day when Sgt. Norm Rabek, the head of the radio section, spotted me and came over.

"The radio section is moving to Linz tomorrow, Zeb," he said. "We're going to set up a radio network and we need another operator. This will be a good opportunity for you to get some practice using Morse code. The bonus is you'll be able to get away from your good friend, Sgt. Colombresi. Would you like to come with us?"

I always liked Sgt. Rabek. He was intelligent and fair to all his men. He was an expert in ham radio communication and never pulled his rank on anybody.

"Count me in, Sergeant," I said.

"I knew you'd say yes," he said, smiling. "By the way, your sergeant's stripes will be here tomorrow."

Morelli was also getting his sergeant's stripes. We celebrated that night by raising a few more glasses of schnapps.

The stripes were long overdue. We had been performing the duties of a sergeant for over a year, but we'd had so many transfers from the artillery companies because of the Battle of the Bulge, all with sergeant's stripes, that the Table of Organization was overloaded and we had to wait until some of them were transferred out of the company

By the time we left Steyr, the Russians on the other side of the river had become much more obnoxious. Not only were they increasing their potshots at the Germans swimming across the Enns every night, but they were actually shooting at the American troops who were swimming in the river on our side. There were several close calls when some of our men narrowly escaped being shot. The Russians thought this was hilarious. They sat on a high bluff across the river. We could hear them yelling and laughing, especially when they shot very close to our men. They were drunk most of the time and apparently that was their game.

We had an anti-aircraft unit with 40mm guns in Steyr at the time. They hadn't shot off their guns in a long time. One day when the Russians were especially numerous up on the bluff, up to their old game of firing indiscriminately at our men, the anti-aircraft unit positioned three of their 40mm guns along the bank of the river and let go with a few salvos aimed halfway up the bluff. There must have been at least one hundred Russians up there drinking vodka and shooting at our men in the water that day. They didn't stop when they saw the 40s go into position. Apparently, they assumed the anti-aircraft men were only bluffing.

It required only a few shells and the entire bank, where the Russians were sitting so cockily a few minutes before, caved in, tossing all of them into the river with a mighty splash. The 40s were hauled out of there in a big hurry and hidden in garages not far from the river.

A formal protest was lodged by the Russian commander and an investigative team was sent by General Whitman. By then the guns had been cleaned so well, they looked as though they hadn't been fired for months. The Russian commander was notified that the renegade gunners couldn't be found. To prevent another such incident, security measures were tightened and the Russians were asked to do the same.

After that, the Russians did not shoot as often, but there was still some sporadic firing from their side for months. The river's edge was finally declared off limits for our troops.

We took off to Linz with a minimum of radio equipment. Sgt. Rabek set up our station and we joined a network that covered Bavaria and Austria. At that time, it was strongly believed that many of the elite German SS troops were planning to regroup at a redoubt in the Berchtesgaden area, the site of Hitler's Eagle's Nest. Nothing of the sort ever happened, but we checked into the network every two hours as a precaution. The rest of the time we were on our own, roaming throughout the city, hiking, and just goofing off.

We were quartered in a large room with bunk beds in an office building that appeared fairly new. The lights were left on continuously and so was the radio. The American Army had already set up a radio station for the GIs called "Luncheon in Munchen," Munchen being the German name for Munich. We quickly adapted to sleeping with all the lights on, along with the radio blaring out our favorite music all night. We ate with an antitank unit that was permanently stationed in Linz. And the crowning aspect of our stay in Linz was the total lack of contact with Headquarters Company or Colombresi for one solid month. It was heaven.

After a month, however, Sgt. Rabek thought it would be the wise to contact Headquarters Company to see what future plans were developing.

"What the hell are you guys doing in Linz?" Majchack exclaimed over the phone. "We've been looking all over Austria and Bavaria, wondering where the devil you men went. You're not supposed to be in Linz."

"What do you mean we're not supposed to be in Linz?" Sgt. Rabek countered. "We had orders from Division Headquarters to go to Linz and join a radio network that covered Bavaria and Austria. That's exactly what we did."

"Pack up your equipment immediately and return to Steyr on the double," Majchack said. "We're moving out to Westheim, just outside of Augsburg, Germany, within a few days. It was mighty lucky that you called."

We didn't think we were so lucky. That was the end of our beautiful sojourn in Linz, Austria. We moved back to Steyr and a few days later we were in pup tents in the woods outside of Westheim. The billeting personnel had forgotten to arrange quarters for us. What the hell! This was the army. We were used to SNAFUs.

The first night we were in the woods, we were hit by the worst thunder and lightning storm I had ever experienced. The rain poured down so heavily we were swamped within thirty minutes. Thunder boomed out like 155mm howitzers, while lightning split the blackness of the forest in frightening streaks. It was just as bad as any artillery barrage we had ever heard. Morelli and I got out of our pup tents and sat on the wet ground.

"It would be ironic to get through combat without a scratch, just to get knocked off by lightning, Zeb," he said, sitting there morosely, water-soaked.

"Unfortunately, that's exactly what can happen," I answered.

Trees were crashing all around us. There was no doubt about it, it was a frightening storm and no time to be out in the woods like a bunch of scared boy scouts.

In the middle of the storm, around three o'clock in the morning, Colonel Wofford's tent blew down. Now that was a real catastrophe. There was more hollering and swearing than you could ever imagine. That was the worst thing that happened to Wofford during the entire war. We were amazed he wasn't awarded, at the very least, a cluster for his previous Silver Star that he had received for his actions on May 5. Three hours later, when the storm had ended we had to stand at attention, under the watchful, scowling eyes of Colonel Wofford, while his officers gave us a lecture and a demonstration on the proper way to erect a tent for the commanding officer of an infantry regiment. There was a lot of snickering going on among the enlisted men during the demonstration with a lot of mean looks thrown our way by all the poor officers suffering the humiliation of the damned. Colonel Wofford allowed the snickering to continue without comment.

A few days later, we moved into a neat white house with a picket fence in Westheim, near a huge iron cross on a hill. It was the home of an artist. He asked Kaputt if he would be permitted to live in the basement with his wife, two children, and his maid. We never found out how he managed to get through such a devastating war in such good circumstances.

Kaputt agreed to that arrangement, but stated the artist would have to paint the lieutenant's portrait in return for that favor. Every day thereafter, Kaputt sat for the artist for several hours, smoking his pipe. He thought the pipe made him look professorial and therefore, more intelligent. We all thought it would take more than a pipe to do that. We were quite happy with that arrangement because the Lieutenant was out of our hair for a considerable length of time, sitting there trying to look intelligent.

Now that the radio network had been dismantled, the chickenshit began in earnest.

We started with the basic elements of dry firing. We formed teams of two men each. One of the men lying prone with his rifle on a support would aim at a target that was pinned to a box. The second man would sit on the box with a bull's eye on a paddle. The bull's eye was pierced in the center by a hole through which the man could insert a pencil and make a dot. When the bull's eye appeared to be in the center of the target, the rifleman would holler out, "Mark." A dot would be made through the bull's eye and the whole procedure would then be repeated two more times. To be successful, the three dots would have to be close enough to be covered by a dime. Then the two men would change places.

We did this all day for two solid weeks. Of course, this was pure chickenshit of the highest order. We then finished up with a week on the firing range. I suppose the big shots figured that by then, if we had to fight Russia, we would be ready.

Kaputt's portrait was finally completed. We told him how remarkably well the artist had captured his basic intelligence and western individuality.

"Do you really thing so?" Kaputt said, standing there looking at the painting admiringly as he rubbed his chin and smoked his pipe, still trying to capture that look of intelligence.

"Absolutely, Lieutenant," Morelli said. "And did you notice how he made you look just slightly cross-eyed to give you that look of confusion you usually had on your face when we were on a mission?"

"How would you like to lose your stripes, Morelli?" Kaputt said.

Kaputt had not received his Silver Star yet. The fact that it wasn't in the painting was such a disappointment to the lieutenant. Sgt. Brawley, after viewing the painting when Kaputt wasn't there, said he was going out to get drunk and then come back and puke on it, but he never carried out his threat. Some of the other men said worse things about it. After several days of viewing, the portrait mysteriously disappeared and the comments ceased.

Our Headquarters Company was soon transferred to Bad Worishofen, a health spa, and we were quartered in what was supposed to be a luxurious hotel. It was pleasant but not luxurious. Life settled down to a monotonous level. Most of us never got up for reveille. One of the sergeants would stand in front of the two or three men who did show up and yell out the standard response at roll call, "All men present and accounted for." That was the high point of the day. It was a pleasant little town, but there was simply nothing to do. One day Edwin Doyle, who also recently got his sergeant stripes, decided to call up the billeting officer in Garmisch-Partenkirchen. This was a resort center in the Bavarian Alps that was taken over by the American Army and used as a rest and recreational center.

"This is Capt. Smith calling from 5th Regimental Headquarters, Captain," Doyle said, lowering his voice to the proper authoritative level. "I'm sending three men to Garmisch on a three day pass starting this Friday and I'd like you to roll out the red carpet for them. They have been working diligently here in Bad Worishofen and need some time off badly. Can that be arranged?"

The billeting officer was happy to accommodate our Capt. Smith. We then went to the company clerk, Corporal Majchack, who gave us a three day pass signing the captain's name himself. At that time, I had been driving a lieutenant around on various errands. He had told me that I could sign his name on a trip ticket anytime I wanted a jeep for my personal use. He didn't need me that weekend. When Friday rolled around, I signed out a jeep and Morelli, Doyle, and I took off for Garmisch. We each had a private room in a beautiful hotel, the

Riessersee, nestled at the base of towering mountains. The brochure in our rooms described our accommodations as follows: "Unser Haus bietet neben gemutlichen zimmern mit Bad und WC, balkon und Telefon, zwei rustikale restaurants, eine 'Minibar', sowie eine Terrasse mit einmaligem Blick auf den See und das Zugspitzmassiv."

We ate the best possible food prepared by German chefs and served by pretty German frauleins. We toured the surrounding area, visiting Hitler's Eagle's Nest in Berchtesgaden, Mad King Ludwig's Linderhof Palace in the Graswang Valley, and Oberammergau, the site of the yearly Passion Play.

When Sunday rolled around, we hated to leave. We hated it so much, we decided to stay another day, even though we then would be considered AWOL.

When we got back to the company area in Bad Worishofen late Monday night, we were surprised to find that nobody knew or cared that we had been gone an extra day.

Doyle imitated our fictitious Capt. Smith again on Wednesday and we repeated our trip to Garmisch. We stayed in the same hotel and enjoyed another splendid weekend. When Sunday came around, all too quickly, we again voted to stay another day, keeping our fingers crossed.

When we got back to Bad Worishofen, nobody even asked us where we had been. Everybody, apparently, was involved in his own little world and didn't give a damn whether we were here, there, or anywhere. That made us feel very confident.

We decided to play our game a third time, knowing that the risk was getting greater. Doyle was successful once again in getting rooms for us in the same hotel. All of us got our three day passes signed by Majchack. I went down to the motor pool and signed out another jeep. Off we went, happy as a bunch of beagles chasing a rabbit. On Sunday, naturally, we again voted to stay an extra day. Unfortunately, Monday was payday and that is the one day of the month that everybody has to be accounted for. When our names were called out with no response, we were automatically declared AWOL. Colombresi was pleased. He went down to the motor pool immediately and found that I had signed out a jeep illegally. He became extremely pleased.

We were confined to quarters for one month and threatened with the loss of our stripes. We felt that was a minor price to pay for three magnificent consecutive weekends. We felt like regular, seasoned army men, soldiers who had learned to utilize every moment at our disposal, legally or illegally. We proved to ourselves what we knew all along, the greater the risk involved, the greater the excitement and enjoyment. At this time, we began to live like officers and gentlemen.

Shortly after these episodes, Headquarters Company was transferred to permanent army barracks, called a kaserne, located in Augsburg, about twenty kilometers west of Munich. The local opera company had already reorganized and Morelli, Doyle, and I began to go to their performances every night. Each production was staged on six consecutive nights, and we attended them all. "The Marriage of Figaro," by Mozart, and "Die Fledermaus," by Strauss were the best and most enjoyable.

Within a few months after the war, the black market was beginning to flourish. All of us quit smoking because we were able to sell our cigarettes for fifty dollars a carton. That price was a great incentive. Being involved in the black market was a dangerous activity. An automatic court-martial was the consequence of being caught. We only sold our own cigarettes, but many of the men in the line companies who were more daring and willing to take a greater risk, sold all kinds of army equipment and supplies, such as blankets, clothing, boots, food, guns, and anything else they could get their hands on. Even the high brass was involved in such activities. There were huge camps of displaced persons throughout Augsburg. These DPs were actively involved in all aspects of this illicit trade.

It was about this time that Bob Marshall came into our company as a replacement. He was a short guy with a glib tongue and a quick smile.

"I'll take your cigarettes off your hands for thirty-five bucks a carton," he said smiling. "I'll sell them downtown for fifty bucks and you guys will avoid the risk of being caught. I'll get fifteen bucks for my efforts, which I believe is fair. Is that a deal?"

We all agreed it was fair. We got one carton of cigarettes every week from the army, along with one bottle of schnapps once a month. The extra money came in handy.

Bob hustled like this for several months. He carried around huge sums of money and began to smoke expensive cigars. Where he got them, we didn't know or care. He began to act more and more like Jimmy Cagney in one of those gangster movies. He was very helpful. If there was anything anybody needed, he would get it immediately and be most happy to do so for the right amount of money.

One night he was caught red-handed in the act of selling his merchandise. By then he had managed to buy a jeep and his business had mushroomed. The OSS arrested him with two hundred and fifty thousand dollars in his pockets and money belt. The jeep was loaded with everything you could think of.

That's the end of Bob Marshall, we thought, the greatest pfc entrepreneur black marketeer in Bavaria. And it *was* the end of *Private First Class Robert Marshall,* but not the end of *Bob Marshall, Mr. Slick, himself.*

Two weeks to the day after his arrest, he came back to our company area wearing a second lieutenant's bar on his collar, a smile bigger than ever spread out on his face.

"You know what you get for impersonating an officer, Bob?" I said to him as soon as I spotted him.

"Salute, my dear boy, salute, or I'll have your ass up on a court-martial for not showing proper respect to this uniform," he said.

He was laughing and stomping around, enjoying our befuddlement to the maximum. He lit up a cigar and puffed away.

"These are real, boys," he said, pointing to his lieutenant's bars. "I'm not kidding. Now if you peasants gather around, I'll tell you an interesting story. You all know that the OSS arrested me in the middle of a big transaction. After questioning me, they realized that I knew all the big-time operators in the black market, including all the DPs, the GIs, the Jews, and a lot of the top brass in the army they wanted to catch. So they offered me a job to work for them as an undercover agent and gave me a commission to boot. Here I am, a second lieutenant and all you low-scum bastards better salute. Who said crime doesn't pay?"

While he was laughing and dancing around like a clown, he puffed himself into a big cloud of smoke. We lost a black marketeer and gained a second lieutenant. That would make any army man jump with joy.

Morelli, Doyle, and I each took a two week furlough to England and Scotland and had an excellent time acting like typical American tourists. When Doyle got back, he somehow managed to get the job of heading the Regimental Information and Education Office. There were many opportunities opening up for the GIs to go to various colleges and universities and even brewery schools throughout the continent of Europe. The only trouble was that most of the guys were shacked up with their frauleins and refused to trade sex for education. The men who were shacked up were easily recognized because they all had scabies and were scratching all the time. Morelli, Doyle and I were among the minority who weren't scratching. Because of this epidemic of scabies, Capt. Davis gave the order that everybody had to sleep in a sleeping bag full of DDT. This didn't have any effect on the scabies mite, but it made Capt. Davis feel very good. So what if DDT was toxic? He gave an order and it was dutifully carried out.

Doyle called me up one day from the I and E Office where he was acting out the part of the captain of the imperial guard. He loved his new position, but was ready to move on to more interesting activities.

"I've got a great deal for you, Zeb," he said. "How would you like to get away from reveille, Colombresi, and all the other crap that goes with that combination?"

"If you've figured out a way without actually killing Colombresi, I'm willing to listen."

"I'm sending myself to Shrivenham, England. The army has set up an American University for all the GIs in Europe who want to go and I need someone I can trust to take my place here at the Regimental I and E Office. What do you say?"

"How can I refuse a deal like that?" I answered. "When are you planning to leave?"

"In two weeks," he said. "Come on over and I'll show you the ropes."

What a deal! I had my own office and the captain in charge checked in only once a month. I found a man in Headquarters Company who could type and we were in business. Now it was my turn, finally, to act the part of the captain of the imperial guard.

All kinds of scholastic opportunities throughout Europe came down from Divisional I and E. It was my job to fill the quotas. This wasn't an easy task because many of the men in the line companies refused to leave their German girlfriends. They were trying to catch up on all the sex they had missed during combat. Therefore, I was forced to raid Headquarters Company. I knew most of the men personally and could fit them more easily into the various educational opportunities that presented themselves.

Within one month I had sent at least fifty men from our company off to school. I even managed to send some of the guys who were scratching the most. That required a strenuous selling job.

One day there was a rather timid knock on the office door. The little runt himself, Sgt. Colombresi, was there, looking somewhat apologetic.

"Zebrowsk," he said, hesitating, "Capt. Davis, he senda me here ta talka ta you, you unnerstanda?"

"What can I do for you, Sgt. Colombresi?" I asked politely.

"I only gotta fifity mena left in da çompany an' I'ma askin' you, in facta, I'ma beggin' you, pleasa don'ta senda any mora my mena from da Headquarters Company ta school. Dey smarta enough already, you unnerstanda, pleasa."

"I can't promise you, Sgt. Colombresi," I said, "that I won't send any more men from Headquarters Company to school for one simple reason. If Division I and E ever found out about such an arrangement, I wouldn't have this job very long. Furthermore, these are opportunities that come only once in a lifetime and these schools were set up by the army for all the GIs who want to go. I'll try to send more men from the line companies, but most of them are shacked up and refuse to go. You must understand my problem. Division I and E gets on my back if I don't fill my quota. But I'll do my best to help you."

"I unnerstan', Zebrowsk," Sgt. Colombresi said, sadly. "Buta pleasa, remember whata I aska you. OK?"

One week later, I got the notice of a new Army University starting up in Biarritz, France. I had a terrible time getting enough men to go there even though it was a splendid resort center on the bay of Biscay near the Spanish border.

I called up Morelli.

"You have to go with me, Morelli," I said, imploringly. "This is a fantastic opportunity. Biarritz is in the same area that Hemingway used in his first novel, "The Sun Also Rises," and I promise you won't regret it."

"Sign me up, Zeb," Morelli said. "You don't have to convince me anymore. But will Capt. Davis let us go?"

"We can't take a chance letting him review the applications," I said. I told him about Colombresi's visit.

"Is there any way we can get around Capt. Davis?" Morelli asked, knowing the answer already.

"Only one way," I answered, 'and that's the same way we got the jeep to go to Garmisch. I'll have to forge his signature. Are you willing to risk your stripes?"

"Nothing risked, nothing gained," Morelli said. "Sign the damn applications and we'll have to suffer the consequences."

"Or the pleasures that are in store for us if we succeed," I said.

I made out the applications. Division I and E approved them within a few days. I found a willing replacement for my position as head of Regimental I and E, which was not difficult to do. All the preparations were in place, finally, and we only had to wait a few more days.

We were planning on one thing to ensure our escape from the confines of Headquarters Company and that was the element of timing. Capt. Davis usually arrived in the company area at eight o'clock in the morning. The truck that I arranged to take us to the train station was scheduled to arrive at six. There was plenty of time. Now if only we could trust them to stick to their schedules.

On D-Day, at quarter to six, Morelli and I and a few other men from the line companies were waiting for the truck when a jeep pulled up next to us and our hearts nearly stopped as Capt. Davis jumped out.

"Where are you men going?" he asked, returning our salute briskly.

"We're off to Biarritz American University in Biarritz, France, Captain, sir," I said smartly, standing rigidly at attention, but quaking in my boots.

"Oh, you are, are you?" he said, as we stood there half-paralyzed, ready to be hauled off to the brig at any moment.

He hesitated a moment, as if he was going to ask for our papers.

"Well, carry on," he said.

He turned and walked away. We watched him disappear into the kaserne as the truck pulled up to take us to the train station.

"Get the hell out of here as fast as you can, soldier," I yelled to the driver.

We pulled out of the company area with tires screaming, away from Capt. Davis, away from Sgt. Colombresi, away from Headquarters Company. Fortunately, the train was on time and we were finally heading towards Biarritz.

Chapter 15

Biarritz

It took five days to get to Biarritz. We went to Frankfurt, then to Paris, Bordeaux, and lastly Biarritz, the gem of the Bay of Biscay. Morelli and I were billeted in a private hotel not far from the shore, the Hôtel de la Rotonde. We each had a private room on the third floor with a built-in douche bowl, where we washed our socks. Every morning we were awakened by an organ grinder playing music with the assistance of his monkey. Unfortunately, the monkey reminded me of Sgt. Colombresi. This detracted from the enjoyment of the music. After awhile, I gradually lost the relationship in my mind as Headquarters Company faded into the background and we became more and more involved with our work in Biarritz.

I signed up for chemistry, physics, and harmony. My advisor, Capt. Norris, a pleasant, patient man, looked at my list of subjects and shook his head.

"You know, Sergeant," he said, pointing out the window of his office, "Biarritz is a famous resort center on the Bay of Biscay."

"Yes, I know that, sir," I said.

"And I assume you realize how fortunate you are to be here," he continued.

"Yes, I certainly do," I said. "It's almost like paradise after what we've been through."

He looked out the window. He was in no hurry to get his point across.

"People used to come from all over the world to relax and

consort with all the high-priced prostitutes who were stabled in all the luxurious villas you see along the shore," he said, still shaking his head as he looked over my list of courses for a second time.

"Yes, I've aware of the past history of this resort," I said. "But I'm planning to go to Dartmouth College and take a pre-med course. Professor Scarlett, the chairman of the chemistry department at Dartmouth is also serving as head of the chemistry department here. I thought I'd get a jump start on my college training."

"There's plenty of time to do that later," Capt. Norris said. "I've looked over your record in the army and the test scores you've received at Fort McClellan, and I can assure you that you will have no problems with the work here or at Dartmouth. You'll probably never get back to Biarritz the rest of your life and you'll learn to regret working your tail off on those three difficult subjects you've chosen. Just let me make a few changes and I promise you that you'll be thankful you followed my suggestions. In fact, you'll be very thankful the rest of your life when you think of Biarritz in the future."

We shot the bull for awhile longer. He finally changed my courses to Twentieth Century Literature, Conversational French, and Music Appreciation. Capt. Norris was right. I remain forever in his debt. I had a wonderful time in Biarritz with Morelli and all my other friends. Homework was never overwhelming. Since I had already been exposed to everything on my course list before I had entered the army, my studies were a breeze. I managed to get an A in each subject without too much effort. Morelli studied Psychology 1, Sociology 1, and Elementary German and managed to do the same.

All of us became friendly with the tavern keeper across the street from our hotel. We quickly developed the habit of drinking a glass of wine after supper before going back to our rooms to study. After a few weeks, we also began meeting at noon for a bull session and another glass of wine. The tavern keeper offered to prepare a black market midnight supper of veal and eggs for us after the tavern closed and we accepted readily. We had a glass of wine at that time, too. That was not counting the wine we drank on the boardwalk, while watching some of the whores lying on the beach in their skimpy bikinis. By the time we left Biarritz, our wine intake had increased dramatically. What we had done is substitute wine for coffee as a social drink. This could have been disastrous for us if we had continued to do this. But we left France after three months and never drank wine again while in the army. In Germany, it was back to beer.

Going to class in Biarritz was always a great pleasure because it meant walking along the beach for a good distance. We were there in October, November, and December of 1945. The air had gotten a little chilly and invigorating, especially at night. During the day it was still pleasantly warm.

There were always some big breakers coming in. Occasionally, when it stormed, the sea was treacherous, the water hitting the rocks with what sounded like the rolling and crashing of thunder, inundating the walk areas with a heavy spray. At the end of the beach, there was a wide stone wall with steep stairs that led up between the villas out to the street. It was difficult to believe that all those villas once occupied by royalty and the very rich ended up being occupied by whores and that prostitution gradually became the main business in Biarritz. At least that was what we were told. Prostitution was flourishing with all the GIs there, too.

At night the atmosphere was magnificent, crisp and clean smelling, heavy with the scent of the ocean. Far out to the left as you faced the sea, the shore curved in a wide arc. We could see the lights from the villages of Spain. San Sebastian was not far from there.

The border town in France was Hendaye, where all of us went one weekend for an all-night dance thrown by the communists. The favorite dance was the jitterbug. Scudder proceeded to get piss-assed drunk, and it was about six in the morning when the dance finally broke up and we woke up the landlady of a rooming house to rent several rooms. We slept all day and got back to Biarritz by bus in time for Sunday supper and to do what homework was necessary. The trip was not worth the trouble, especially for Scudder. It took him three days to dry out.

One week later, Scudder was pounding on my door at three o'clock in the morning.

"You're drunk again, Scudder," I mumbled, half asleep. "Go back to your room and let me sleep in peace. I've got an exam in the morning."

"I just got fucked, Zeb," Scudder said. He staggered around the

161

room, looking worried.

I yawned and stretched.

"So?" I grumbled. "Am I supposed to jump up and down and clap my hands?"

"I was with one of those whores downtown," Scudder said.

"That's stupid," I said. "And now you're going to tell me you didn't use a rubber."

"You're right," he said. "I didn't."

"I didn't realize you were such a jerk, Scudder," I said.

"I was drunk," he said.

"Well, what the hell do you want me to do about it?" I said.

"Will you come down to the pro station with me?" Scudder said. He started to cry.

"You don't need me," I said. "There's a medic on duty there twenty-four hours a day. He knows how to give you a pro."

"Please, Zeb," Scudder said. "I'm so goddamn drunk I can barely stand up."

To prove this last statement he promptly fell down.

"Come on downtown with me," he continued to plead as he lay on the floor, struggling awkwardly to get up.

He finally made it to his feet and stood swaying in the middle of the room.

Scudder knew that I was planning to go into medicine after I got out of the army. I looked at him. He was pitiful, his clothes dirty and disheveled. He staggered over to the bed and sat down, holding his head, crying.

"Wait a minute while I get dressed, you horse's ass," I said.

We walked to the pro station which was downtown in the center of Biarritz. I walked, Scudder staggered. On the way he fell several times. I waited patiently, letting him get up by himself.

The medic was a sour son-of-a-bitch who didn't bother to look up as we came in. He pretended to be very busy as he shuffled papers around on his desk.

"Here's a customer for you," I said. "He just fucked one of those wonderful vendors of ecstasy you see wandering down the street and he needs a pro."

"There it is on the counter," the medic said sarcastically, "just waiting for any loose cannon to stroll in."

I hesitated.

"Take it into one of those cubicles along the wall and have him give it to himself," he said impatiently, obviously upset because we had interrupted his routine.

"He's too damn drunk to give it to himself," I said. "You can see that for yourself, if you're not blind."

"I'm not going to do it for him," the medic said. "I'm too busy checking out my supplies."

"You don't look that busy," I said.

"Why don't you just go fuck yourself?" the medic said.

"Are you always this nice?" I said. "Your mother would certainly be proud of you, serving with such distinction in the United States Army."

He didn't bother to answer me.

I took Scudder into one of the cubicles, put on the rubber gloves, and cleaned his dick with a special antiseptic. I squirted the entire tube of the chemical prophylactic into his urethra and told him to hold it.

"I'll never forget this," Scudder said, still sobbing.

"Neither will I," I said.

I took him back to the hotel and put him in his bed. It was five o'clock. I slept until six, showered, and went to the mess hall for breakfast. Morelli was already there waiting for me.

"Did you sleep well?" he asked.

"Like a rock," I answered.

Chapter 16

A Shot in the Dark

The water was dripping off the roof in two different places, *crack-thump, crack-thump,* the two sounds nearly together. Tulley lay on the narrow bed and listened in the darkness, afraid. Sometimes the sounds would get mixed up, the rhythm gone, and the rain outside, blown by the wind against the window, would drown them out completely. He felt the muscles in his legs tighten up and ache with fatigue. Then the sounds would come back louder, *crack-thump,* filling the room, sounding in his head, beating against his brain, *crack-thump.* And all the while he continued to feel the terrible burning in the middle of his belly. He turned on his side and held his breath every time it started, his muscles tight. Then he'd let out his breath slowly and he'd roll over on his back, his body wet beneath the blankets.

"Here, this will make you feel better, soldier," the woman said.

"What are you doing?" Tulley said. "Leave me alone. I don't want anything to make me feel better."

He felt a sting in his left arm.

"Dammit," he yelled out. "I asked you what you're doing?"

"I just gave you a shot," the woman said, quietly.

"Are you a nurse?"

"Yes, I am."

Tulley saw a blur of white.

"Here, Sgt. Tulley, put this mask on."

It was a man's voice.

"What mask?" Tulley asked. "I don't want a mask. Why should

I put on a mask? The war's over, anyway. I threw my gas mask away a long time ago."

"This is to make you sleepy so you won't feel anything," the man persisted.

"Take that damn mask away," Tulley said. "It stinks. What are you trying to do, kill me?"

Crack-thump, Tulley heard it again. Where the hell is it coming from?

He saw the girl standing behind the bar, hands on her hips, smiling. She was pretty. Her thin dress barely concealed her body.

"Did you hear that sound, Anna?" Tulley asked her.

"Crack-thump," Anna said. "Yes, I hear it."

"What did you say?" Tulley said, confused.

"Crack-thump," she said again. "It's your American friend, Blake, Sgt. Blake. He came with you."

"What about Sgt. Blake?" Tulley said. "Is he here at the hospital?"

"No, he's not here now," the nurse said. "He stayed with you all day until after the operation. He finally went back to the barracks. He was falling over, he was so tired."

"Sgt. Blake?" the girl behind the bar asked. "He's here. The two of you came together, don't you remember?"

Crack-thump, Tulley heard it again. Why doesn't it stop?

"Your American friend, Blake, is drunk," Anna said. "He keeps hitting the table with both hands, *crack-thump*. He thinks I'll bring him another schnapps if he keeps hitting the table like that. But he's too drunk."

He looked over at Blake. He was sitting at another table in the far corner in a semi-stupor.

"He is drunk," Tulley said. "Don't give him any more to drink no matter how hard he hits the table. I'll have a hard time getting him back to the kaserne as it is."

"You'll never make it," Anna said. "He's already too drunk to walk. You'll have to sleep over."

Anna gave the bar a couple of swipes with a cloth.

Crack-thump.

Blake was at it again, his left hand slapping the table with a sharp crack, while his right hand in a tightly closed fist, followed quickly with a loud thump.

"Both of you can stay over in my room upstairs," Anna said. "You can leave early in the morning before it gets light so you won't get caught by the MPs. Did you bring any cigarettes like you promised?"

"Yes," Tulley said, patting his pockets. "I've got plenty of cigarettes."

"Crack-thump," the second lieutenant said.

"What the hell is going on?" Tulley said, startled.

The second lieutenant appeared irritated.

"Pay attention," he yelled out.

Tulley raised himself on one elbow and looked out through the window at the black night. The rain was a sharp splatter against the glass and a branch, moving with the wind, kept scraping against it.

Crack-thump.

The sound came again above the wind and the sweeping rain. He turned to lie on his side, his face screwed up with pain.

"Are you listening, soldier?" the second lieutenant said. "This information could save your ass in combat."

"The war is over," Tulley laughed. "What the hell are you talking about?"

"Now listen to what I'm saying," the second lieutenant kept on, ignoring Tulley's remark. "When someone's firing at you, you can hear the bullet make a snapping sound in the air as it passes close by, if you're lucky, 'crack', just like the sound of the word. Are you listening, soldier, or am I talking into thin air?"

"I'm listening," Tulley said. "What do you want from me? I'm listening."

"Then you'll hear the sound of the rifle, just like a thump in the distance. The closer you are to the guy firing at you, the closer the two sounds will be together. *Crack-thump.* Do you understand that, soldier?"

"I already know that," Tulley said. "I learned that in basic training. *Crack-thump.* It sounds just like the rain dripping off the roof and the way Blake was hitting the table when he wanted more schnapps. By the way, where the hell is Blake?"

"He was here all day," the nurse said. "I already told you that. He's gone to get some sleep. He'll be back. He was very worried about you."

"What about Anna?" Tulley asked. "The German girl behind the bar."

"I don't know anything about a German girl behind the bar or anybody named Anna, or anything about crack-thump. You were hallucinating, Sergeant."

"Hallucinating?" Tulley said, puzzled. "I didn't have that much to drink. If anybody was hallucinating, it must have been Blake. He was stinko last night."

"It was the anesthesia," the nurse said.

"What anesthesia?" Tulley said, surprised. "You've got me all screwed up, do you know that?"

"You were shot in the belly, Sergeant, and the surgeons had to operate on you," the nurse said. "Now try to get some sleep."

"What's this tube in my nose?" Tulley said, ready to yank it out.

"Don't touch that, Sergeant," the nurse said. "That's to keep your stomach empty until you're healed enough to take food by mouth. In a few days, after your intestines start working again and you start to pass gas, the doctor will take it out."

The branches bent with the heavy wind and kept scraping the window. Tulley lay on the bed, wet, shivering, his throat dry and sore, breathing quickly, his eyes wide open, searching the blackness around him.

Crack-thump.

There it was again. He nearly cried out as he felt the sharp stabbing pain in his belly.

He was lying face down against the cool, wet grass and breathing hard.

"They're trying to kill us," Blake said quietly.

He was still shaky from the heavy drinking he had done the night before. They had slept over in Anna's room. It was five in the morning and it was still dark. Tulley and Blake had been warned a number of times about getting back to the kaserne late at night. They were breaking the curfew repeatedly.

About every two or three days, another GI would be found dead

167

on the street in Augsburg, either shot in the head or his throat slit. There were still some dedicated SS troops who were fighting the war on a one to one basis, or some German civilians seeking vengeance.

Tulley pulled on Blake so that he would follow closely as they walked quickly through a section of the city park that was a short cut back to the kaserne. He was beginning to feel sorry that they had gone that way. The bushes in the park provided a hiding place for them from the MPs, but the Germans out to kill an American soldier could hide there, too.

Tulley stopped suddenly. He pushed Blake slowly down to the ground.

"What's the matter?" Blake whispered.

"Shhhh," Tulley said. "I think I hear someone in those bushes up ahead of us, just to the right. Don't move. We'll stay right here and wait for a few minutes. We're in no hurry."

"It's probably just one of the GIs screwing one of the German broads," Blake said.

"No," Tulley said. "Why should they be out here when they could be in a nice warm bed? And I heard a distinct click."

They heard it again, louder now, a sharp clicking, like the sound of the carriage being pulled back on a semi-automatic pistol and then being let go, with a cartridge entering the chamber at the same time.

"Those bastards," Blake said between clenched teeth. "They still want to fight."

"At least some of them do," Tulley said. "We'll wait them out. The MPs patrol this park all the time and those sons-of-bitches will take off like big-ass birds when they see the MPs."

"And we'll end up getting a court-martial for breaking the curfew," Blake said.

"That's better than getting killed. Now keep quiet."

The MPs didn't come.

It was still black and Tulley and Blake couldn't see a thing. There were no more clicks.

"They can't see us," Blake said. "Should we make a run for it?"

"Wait a minute," Tulley said. "There's no hurry. They may not be able to see us, but they could certainly hear us if we make a run for it."

They waited another ten minutes. Everything was quiet.

"Do you think they took off?" Blake asked.

"I doubt it," Tulley said. "I think they're waiting for us to make a move. It's going to start getting light soon and then it'll get real hairy for everybody."

Another ten minutes went by.

"Listen, Blake," Tulley said. "I'm going to throw a rock to the right. When I do and they start firing, you run to the left behind them. If you stumble, you're a dead man. When you get past them about twenty yards, you throw another rock to your left and I'll take off. Do you think you're sober enough to that without getting killed?"

"Yes," Blake said quickly. "Just lying here and waiting isn't doing us any good. Tell me when."

Tulley threw the rock and Blake took off as if a stroke of lightning had hit him in the ass. Four blasts of gun fire sounded from the bushes ahead of them, but they were firing in the wrong direction. From the flashes, Tulley was sure there were only two snipers. He heard Blake's feet pounding on the ground in the distance as he fired three rounds from his Luger to cover up the sound. He heard a grunt from one of the men. He quickly crawled away from his bush before they had a chance to fire back. He was glad he did because they opened up with a burp gun. He heard the slugs rake the spot where he had been a few moments before.

Everything was quiet again.

Tulley knew that Blake had made it safely when he heard the second stone. He took off, feet pounding, as he heard the bullets snapping, "crack," all around him, with the following "thump" of the pistols. The two sounds were almost simultaneous. He knew the snipers weren't too far away. They must have figured out his strategy because they were firing in the opposite direction of the second stone. Run, he said to himself, run with all your might on that sweet-smelling grass that will cover your grave if they get you, run with tired legs dragging, chest heaving, weary body pumping, just like you did hundreds of times before in combat.

He felt a sudden stabbing pain in his belly and he knew that he had caught one and he was scared. He hit the ground hard, swearing under his breath, as a terrible spasm gripped his body.

He heard the Germans yell out something and then the pounding of feet as they ran deeper into the woods. A jeep pulled up with a loud screeching noise as it skidded to a stop. Two MPs jumped out. Tulley was lying on the edge of the road in the glare of the headlights, holding onto his belly, still swearing.

Blake ran over to him.

"I caught one in the belly," Tulley said, gasping with pain. "We nearly made it. Are you all right?"

"Yeah, yeah," Blake said. "I'm all right. Never mind me."

The MPs came over.

"What the hell are you guys doing out here in the park at this hour?" one of them said angrily.

"Trying to stay alive," Tulley said. "Thanks for asking."

"Can't you see he's been shot in the belly?" Blake said. "We have to get him to the hospital right away. You can ask your questions later."

The MPs got him out fast. Tulley was under the knife within an hour.

The next day the surgeon, Dr. Barker, came into Tulley's room smiling. He was holding a large, silver, non-regulation belt buckle.

"I thought you'd like this as a souvenir, sergeant," he said. "It's all bent to hell where the 9mm slug hit it, but that's what saved your life. You're one tough son-of-a-bitch."

"Thanks," Tulley said weakly. "I thought the war was over three months ago. Take this fucking tube out of my nose, will you, Doc?"

He turned over on his side and went to sleep. He was smiling.

Chapter 17

Raids

We got back from Biarritz at midnight, December 31, 1945, after a five-day trip on the train. It was cold and there was a mixture of snow and sleet coming down. Augsburg looked mighty dreary after Biarritz. Morelli and I stumbled off to bed exhausted. At three in the morning, I woke up suddenly with somebody shaking the hell out of my shoulder.

"If you want a pro, soldier, you came to the wrong man," I said without turning over. I was sleepy and irritable.

"Get your ass out of bed, Sir Lancelot. We're going on a raid."

There was a staff sergeant scowling at me at the side of the bed. I had never seen him before.

"What the hell kind of raid are you talking about and just who the hell are you? Can't a guy get a little sleep around here?"

I sat up on the edge of the bed, blinking my eyes against the light. I scowled back at him.

"Murdock's the name," he said. "Staff Sergeant Murdock. And for your information, we're raiding a DP camp. Or did you forget all about the displaced people and the flourishing black market around here, the so-called 'enslaved hordes' that Hitler imported from the countries he conquered?"

"As a matter of fact, I did forget," I said. "I even began to feel like a civilian while I was in Biarritz."

"I don't know where Biarritz is," Murdock said. "But I know where you are now, so get moving."

"I can't," I said. "I told you we just got back from Biarritz, France, and I don't have an M1."

"We'll fix that soon enough," Murdock said. "You can draw one from the supply room, along with one clip of ammunition. There are no prima donnas here this morning. Everybody's going on this raid."

"Who's the stupid ass who scheduled a raid on New Year's Day?"

"I did," Murdock said.

"Great idea," I said. "Great idea."

I looked at Morelli who was yawning and stretching.

"Isn't it nice to be back?" he asked in between yawns. "We should have stayed in Biarritz another three months."

Outside it was bitter cold. A wet, drizzly snow was falling and the pavement was slippery. We piled into two-and-a-half-ton trucks and drove out to one of the larger DP camps on the outskirts of Augsburg. My glasses were wet and the street lights were misty puff balls through the lenses.

Morelli came up to me shivering, his nose dripping from the melted snow.

"This is what you call a real homecoming," he said sarcastically. "In Biarritz, I forgot I was in the army."

"It almost looks as if they did this deliberately," I said, "just to remind us how shitty the army really is."

"It's not the army that's shitty, Zeb," Morelli said. "It's the individual shitty guys in the army who have the power to issue shitty orders."

We saw an officer with a second lieutenant's bar on his collar coming towards us.

"Speaking of individual shitty guys," I said, "who's the shithead with the second lieutenant's bar?"

"Some new guy," Morelli said. "You can see he plans to make a big name for himself just by the way he walks. Thank God he wasn't around when we were in combat."

"Somehow he looks familiar," I said.

The lieutenant appeared to be in a hurry.

"You guys all set?" he asked. "We'll fix these slimy black

market pigs once and for all. I have a feeling we'll make a big haul tonight."

He was a short guy with a thin pale face, thin lips and a small mouth, the kind of individual you dislike at first sight. It wasn't just the way he looked, but the way he carried himself that seemed to aggravate everybody. Of course, the fact that he wore a second lieutenant's bar didn't help.

I couldn't remember where I had seen him before.

"At exactly three o'clock, we'll go into this building next to us," the lieutenant said. "I've got some inside information that this is one of the centers of the black market here in Augsburg."

He checked his watch.

"In five minutes," he said.

All the men were ready and at exactly three o'clock we entered the building like a bunch of cockroaches attacking a loaf of bread. There was a foul smell in the hallways, a mixture of human excrement, urine, filthy bodies, and the acrid smell of German tobacco smoke. Real cockroaches scurried along with us in every direction.

"You and you, come with me," the lieutenant said.

He pointed to Morelli and me. I guess he liked the comfort of being surrounded by sergeants. He looked about twenty-four and acted as if he had attended the same acting school as General Patton and General MacArthur.

On entering the building, the lieutenant immediately went to the last room at the end of the hall. Morelli and I assumed this was because of his inside information. He drew his .45, kicked the door down in the best John Wayne tradition, and stood crouched in the doorway with both hands on his pistol.

There was a young woman in bed. She sat up suddenly and was about to scream.

"Don't scream," he warned. "It won't do you any good."

Morelli and I watched him from the doorway. There was a wooden box near the bed. The lieutenant nearly stumbled rushing over to it.

"Where did you get this blanket?" he snarled. He grabbed the army blanket out of the box and threw it on the floor in the center of the room.

"Don't touch my baby," the young woman cried out. "That blanket is for my baby."

The baby started to cry. The young woman jumped out of bed, her night dress up high, her legs showing white for a moment. She hugged the baby to her chest. She looked even more fragile standing there, frightened, starting to cry softly herself.

"That's for my baby," she said again.

"That's too goddamn bad, lady," the lieutenant said hoarsely. "That blanket happens to be army issue."

He moved over to a chest of drawers and started dumping everything out.

"Come on, men, start moving. I didn't take you along for the ride, you know."

I walked past a small cast iron stove with a pipe going through a hole ripped out of the wall. There was a small table near the stove with two candy bars, half a loaf of bread, a dirty coffee pot, and a small frying pan with some old food stuck to it. A crumpled diaper was lying in the corner.

"Did you have some inside information regarding this particular room, Lieutenant?" I said. "We might be on the wrong floor."

The Lieutenant was stomping around the room like a wild animal, throwing things all over the place as he emptied all the drawers. He ignored my question.

"Ah, what do we have here?" he said glowingly, dumping one of the drawers on the floor. "I knew we'd have to find cigarettes somewhere."

He threw three cartons of Camels onto the blanket in the middle of the floor, triumphant at last.

"Where did you get these cigarettes and the army blanket, lady?" he barked out.

The young woman was standing near the wall in the far corner of the room, her back to us, holding the baby close to her and humming softly.

The lieutenant stood there, legs apart, his right hand resting on the butt of his .45, sneering, the Grand Inquisitor.

"I bought them from an American soldier," she said. She didn't turn around to look at him.

The Lieutenant laughed harshly.

"The same soldier who gave you the baby, I bet," he said. "All right, Zebrowski. You and Morelli take this contraband down to the truck."

"Contraband!" Morelli said. The word seemed to explode out of his mouth. "You really want us to take this *contraband*, Lieutenant?"

"I've got a job to do, Morelli," the Lieutenant said, "and I'm going to do it. I can't make any exceptions. I'm just sick to death of these people and the black market crap that we have to put up with."

"Yes, I understand your position," Morelli kept on, "but it seems that the GIs either sell this stuff or give it away in the daytime and then we come around at night in a big raid and take it back. These people are living on the edge of disaster, sir, and have been for years. They are freed slaves."

"Disaster, my ass, Morelli," the Lieutenant said. "I'm in no mood to debate the issue with you. Now take that crap downstairs like I ordered you."

Doors were still being banged open and shut throughout the building and we could hear a lot of people running in the hall. One of the men in our raiding party ran up to the Lieutenant breathless.

"There's a guy downstairs in the basement that I think is the son-of-a-bitch you're looking for, Lieutenant."

The Lieutenant, finally striking gold, followed the GI out of the room as if propelled by a rocket. Morelli and I heard them going down the stairs two at a time.

"That should keep the little shithead occupied for awhile," I said, happy to see him leave the room.

"Thank God," Morelli said.

We gave the blanket and the cigarettes back to the young woman and told her to hide them immediately. We knew we'd be in deep trouble if that little fart of a second Lieutenant found out what we had done. We got out of there fast and went back to the truck.

"Who the hell is that son-of-a-bitch?" Morelli said. "He looks like he'll get his, someday."

"I don't know his name," I said, "but I know I've seen that face somewhere before."

One of the replacements came up to us. He had overheard our

conversation.

"That's Lieut. Kendall," he said. "He used to be in one of the line companies. He was a wonder there, too."

Later on that same day, it finally came to me. It was just outside of Pegnitz. Our platoon had finally caught up with Baker Company when we saw two jeeps drive past with two dead GIs draped over the hoods.

It was a small farming village with a few clusters of cement farmhouses with the strong smell of manure permeating the whole area. There was cow dung mixed with straw piled up in front of each house, ready to be spread on the adjacent fields. Apparently a sniper was hiding somewhere in the village. That's when I first saw Lieut. Kendall with that thin pale face and thin lips. He had that same determined look then that he had on that raid on the DP camp.

He ordered mortars to be set up in the fields at the edge of the village. We sat there in the hot sun and listened to the hollow thumping of the mortars and watched the tired-looking dogfaces crouching over their weapons. The firing didn't stop until the entire village was leveled. Lieut. Kendall stood there the same way he did in that young woman's room, legs apart, thin lips tight against his teeth, his right hand on his gun butt. He looked very satisfied. Then we rode into the village, the vanquishers face to face with the vanquished. All the people of the village were standing outside near their totally demolished houses. There were old ladies with trembling hands entwined with prayer beads, toothless old men with manure on their boots, and young children holding onto their mothers. They were all crying and holding white pieces of cloth.

I could see Lieut. Kendall looking exultant as he rode through the devastated village. I had to look away. The sniper wasn't found.

That night when I was lying on my cot, I closed my eyes. I was very tired. Instead of seeing that magnificent beach in Biarritz, I kept seeing Lieut. Kendall, determined, victorious, thin lips tight against his teeth, right hand resting on the butt of his .45. I saw the fragile young woman again, crying, humming to her baby that she held tightly to her chest, the baby that was fathered by a GI who had given her the candy and the cigarettes.

I was half asleep but I thought I saw a white cloth in the young woman's hand as a sign of surrender.

Chapter 18

The Sound of Drums

Tender as thou lived,
So thou died,
Too holy for sorrow!
No eye can weep
At the homecoming of a heavenly
soul.

Beethoven's Elegiac Song

Ellen walked up the long sloping hill overlooking the sea as the sun cast its last leaping flames across the dimming sky. She watched the wind in little gusts sweep against the tall slender grass, dipping, rising, and swirling itself up the hill ahead of her, as if inviting her up the path she had walked so many times before.

It had been a long time, she thought, and it had been so lonely those empty months since Mac had left. But suddenly, up on the hill, it seemed that it hadn't been so long after all, that Mac had always been there, had never stopped holding her in his arms and whispering to her. Everywhere she turned, she felt his presence. That was why she was constantly drawn to that same spot. Time had no meaning there. It was merely an interval between events in her life that simply evaporated, leaving behind the crystals of those special moments to be relived in her mind again and again.

She reached the top of the hill and stood looking out at the viscid sea that flung itself upon the ground and then sucked back through the rocky shore, leaving behind a sound like the tumult of many voices obscured by a vast distance. And she heard the leaves in their ceaseless dance, rustling and murmuring in response like a soft nocturnal symphony.

These voices seemed to call to Ellen, and she responded with her whole being. The top of the hill, filled with the wind and the smell of the sea, was the past, the past that continually reminded her of the moments that she and Mac had spent together.

There was something about the sea, about the way it overwhelmed the shore with its incessant assault that made her stand there as if in a trance, a helpless young girl, weary, alone, and already lost in the memories of the past, like some wrinkled up old woman. And the power of the water, beating against the rocks, rushing and then drawing back, getting ready for yet another thrust, its strength full and furious, only made her feel more helpless.

It was spring when Mac had left. The whole world was throbbing with a tremendous pulse, a fast and overpowering beat caused by the events of the war. And with the onset of spring again, it was almost agonizing to see the intense green growth leap from the earth, dazzling in the warmth of the bright sun. She remembered Mac's face, nearly lost in the crowd of young men, eager with youthful anticipation, alert, bright, yearning, tinged with the melancholy of departure. The band led the way to the railroad station with music quick and sharp, echoing the tremendous beat of the whole earth, music that gripped your heart enough to make you breathless, enough to make you almost gasp from the throbbing pulsations, enough to frighten you with its inexorable, overwhelming, feverish rhythm.

There was Ellen and spring and the whole earth along with Mac, caught up in the frenzied pounding of the entire universe. It was impossible to escape. It was an immense wave that grabbed them and hurled them into an entirely unknown world, filled with fear and uncertainty.

And then the long, dreary, sad months drifted one after another, tied together like a bow with those brief messages from Mac, it seemed from nowhere, that she tucked away in her mind, while she kept her lonely vigil on the hill overlooking the sea. Spring had gone for the second time since Mac had left and now autumn stealthily

crept in, with its wild torrent of colors and cold winds. This intensi-
fied her sense of loneliness and her underlying sadness.

Ellen walked along the narrow path that skirted the cliff until she
came to a huge rock half-buried in the ground.

"This is our rock, Mac," she had said very seriously, "and
nobody can take it away."

"It's too heavy for anybody to take away," Mac had said, laughing. "It's going to stay right here forever."

"Just like us," she added.

"Yes, just like us," Mac said.

Ellen sat down and drew her knees up, leaning back against the
rock's worn surface. She watched the sun in its final reluctant flight
beyond the rim of the world. It darkened quickly then. She and Mac
had come often to the same rock to watch the sea and the sky em-
brace in their nightly ritual. They'd sit quietly, looking out upon the
water, listening to it rush against the rocks and fall on the sand and
they would tremble while they held each other. It was frightening,
understanding each other so completely, as if they were joined into
one person. It was like standing on the edge of a steep rock and
swaying in a light breeze, a wind that threatened to release you in free
flight, not daring to look down, yet knowing what you'd see if you
did, and then looking down quickly with deep fright filling your mind
as you floated through the air with a final sense of relief.

It was funny, she thought. They'd sit there watching night come
on and everything would seem to slow down. The water would come
in more gently, licking over the glistening rocks almost lazily. When
it fell on the sand, the sound would be softer and would float up to
them slowly, on air heavy with the smell of the sea. Even the sound
of some distant animal would begin quietly and all the other sounds
of the night wouldn't be quick and sharp, but rather blurred and
unending. It was as if the tranquillity of the night was soothing and
calming the agitation of the day. When the night slowed everything
down like that, she'd close her eyes and feel that she was gliding
through the air like a swift bird in the night. Her blood would rush
through her body and pound in her temples until all her muscles
would tremble. And then her flight would end and the earth would
move instead, and she'd see the water and the rocks and the trees

shift rapidly beneath her. She'd get dizzy and open her eyes. She'd look up at Mac and see him looking at her. Her whole body would shudder.

"Ellen," Mac would whisper, "I love you."

He'd hold her tighter and she'd lift her face up to his and feel him bending her back against the rough face of the rock. Then even the sound of the water falling and being sucked back wouldn't reach her anymore.

But now that was all she heard. She opened her eyes and saw that the sea and the sky had joined in their nightly communion. The stars brightened slowly and the sky appeared colder than the sea. She huddled down in her coat as the night air became damp and heavy with mist.

A sound came to her and she was suddenly rigid. It was like a sigh brought to her on the night wind. It came again and her heart was nearly bursting in her chest. She couldn't recognize it at first, but it seemed she had heard it before. She stood up quickly, bracing herself against the huge rock that was cold and rough beneath her hand. Was it the sound of the sea and the wind playing tricks on her senses? She continued to listen, straining against the wind, her whole body alive and vibrant now.

But the sound was not repeated. She turned down the path leading to the bottom of the hill. Far below her she saw the lights of the village, little warm spheres suspended in the coldness of the night. She went down the path slowly and entered the small cottage at the foot of the hill. The room was filled with a soft yellow light. The warm air felt good against her cheeks. She took off her coat and sat at the kitchen table.

Her mother came over and set a steaming cup of hot cocoa in front of her. "I thought you'd like a hot drink," her mother said. "It's colder than usual tonight and I was beginning to worry about you up on the hill."

Ellen stared at the cup for a long time. Tears gradually filled her eyes and a spasm gripped her body. Her lips began to quiver.

"Now, now," her mother said soothingly, touching Ellen's head gently. "Everything's going to be all right, dear. Please drink your cocoa."

"When is he coming, mother?"

Ellen looked down at her cup. Tears streamed down her cheeks, leaving behind their glistening, interlacing paths.

"Eleven tomorrow morning, Ellen," her mother said softly. "Everything has been taken care of."

She put her hand on Ellen's shoulder.

Ellen closed her eyes. She saw once again all those bright, eager faces and heard the band with its fiercely-calling music and she felt the beat of the whole earth within her own body.

She looked at her mother.

"There won't be a...band or anything like that, will there, mother?" Ellen said, crying softly.

"No, dear," her mother said, tears springing quickly to her eyes. "Just drums. Four drums."

Ellen closed her eyes again.

"I hate drums," she whispered, her fists clenched tightly on the table. "I hate drums."

McHugh was coming home at last.

Chapter 19

Redeployment

Life settled down to a monotonous level in the early months of 1946. We were in the Army of Occupation and there wasn't much to do except put up with the chickenshit that seemed to mount higher every day. We tried to rekindle the excitement of the early days after the war but we were losing too many men to redeployment. Morelli, Doyle, and I went back to Hitler's Eagle's Nest for another visit, but even that didn't relieve us of our boredom. At the Eagle's Nest in 1945, some of the big military brass had a sign, "For Field Grade Officers Only," erected at the base, restricting the use of the brass mirrored elevator that Hitler used to go up through the mountain to his retreat. That meant it could be used only by colonels and generals. When we came there a year later, the sign had been removed and we were able to use the elevator even though we were lowly sergeants. The story supplied to us was that General Eisenhower, upon seeing the sign, blew his top and ordered it removed. But the army had made us into a bunch of cynical bastards and we didn't believe the self-glorifying Eisenhower version. We had become so cynical that we believed Eisenhower's greatest victory was the invasion of Great Britain by American troops. As for the sign, we preferred to believe that a biting cartoon by Bill Mauldin in our newspaper, *The Stars and Stripes*, picturing two officers viewing a beautiful scene from a mountain top with the caption, "Is there a scene like this for enlisted men, too?" proved to be too embarrassing for the top brass and that resulted in the removal of the sign.

But we really didn't give a damn about that, either. All of us had already begun to think like civilians. Redeployment was on every-body's mind. Who the hell cared about the officers or what they thought? We knew who had won the war and the civilians in the army were ready to go home. In the army we had been second-class individuals, just expendable cannon fodder. Now, we were ready to assume our rightful place in our society.

The bureaucrats in Washington had figured out a simple way to determine which men were sent home first, and surprisingly enough, the plan worked. Points were awarded for length of service, overseas duty, and for special awards, such as the Purple Heart. Naturally, the older men were the first to go.

Dan Groves, the GI who had covered his genitals with his hel-met the first day we hit the front in Bitche, France, had more points than most of us because of his length of service. If he had been awarded points for fornication, he would have had one hundred times as many. He was loaded with scabies and had an itch to beat all itches. Unfortunately, he received a "Dear John" letter just before he was sent home. His wife had found somebody else to keep her warm while he was fighting the good battle. We did our best to cheer him up but he went into a fit of depression that aggravated his itching severely. He was hospitalized for a number of days with the diagno-sis of "Battle Fatigue." This was eight months after the war had ended. His real problem was sexual fatigue. Dan had been so active sexually after the war that all of us thought he would surely die "in the saddle." He had lost thirty pounds. Being slender to begin with and blessed with a posture that resembled a question mark, he looked like one of the walking dead. We actually took bets on how long he would survive. He looked fragile but had the stamina of a bull. He did survive, but Dan nearly became the first American soldier to die from excessive fornication. This would have looked terrible on his death certificate. We were convinced that redeployment saved his life and spared him that disgrace.

We gradually lost our men through redeployment and it was tough on those left behind. Ruben Densman was one of the first to leave. He got his orders shortly after the war ended. He hitched rides on the Red Ball Express to Frankfurt, preferring to arrange his own travel plans. From there he scrounged a flight to LeHavre. He sailed home shortly thereafter on the Marine Angel hospital ship. We all thought he was sent home early to prevent him from shooting Capt. Mudger for sending him on his last wire mission that ended up with all his crew being shot to hell.

Ed Doyle left in March. We were allowed to take one pistol home. He took his Luger with him and left a beautiful Mauser target pistol with me with explicit instructions. He told me to break it down and send one piece to him every week. I followed his instructions and all the pieces arrived safely at his home in Lynn, Massachusetts. In return for this favor, Doyle agreed to take home a pen and ink sketch for me by George Geissler done in 1920 that I had bought in Garmisch. He admired it so much that I had a difficult time getting it back after I arrived home.

Morelli was offered master sergeant's stripes to entice him to sign up for another six months. He refused the offer and was redeployed a few weeks after Doyle.

I received the same offer when my turn for redeployment came. I refused, too, even though it was tempting to be promoted to the rank of master sergeant at the age of twenty. However, I couldn't think of anything else but going home and getting ready for college.

I was discharged on June 6, 1946, at Fort Dix, New Jersey. Morelli missed the gang so much that within two weeks he was at my door in Thompsonville, Connecticut, for a reunion.

That fall we both started college. It was the beginning of an entirely new life for both of us.

Epilogue

Now, forty-seven years later, I meet with many of my old comrades from Headquarters Company during our 71st Division yearly reunions. We also have mini-reunions among ourselves during the year. The bond that we forged in 1944 through 1946 will only be broken by death.

We are now faced with a new and deadly enemy, just as we had been in World War II. The enemy is no longer the German Army. It is even deadlier. Old age and disease are threatening our diminishing lines but we're trying to hold steady. These twin menaces, hand in hand, are gradually decimating our old troops.

When I take out my old Luger and P-38 for an occasional inspection, cleaning, and reminiscing, all my old friends spring into full action, their faces bold, young, vibrant and full of anticipation just as they were back in 1945 when we first hit the front in Bitche, France.

The air is again charged with that same dangerous excitement that only war can create and I feel the wild beat of the entire universe as it courses through my aging body.

I see Morelli again, getting in and out of his jeep, smiling and flashing his thumbs-up sign. Sam Brawley, grumpy as ever, is growling and muttering under his breath, his lower lip sticking out a mile. The SS trooper, standing tall and fierce in the bright sunlight, is looking at us with audacious contempt after shooting the shocked newspaperman in the chest. Doc Neuman is crouched beside the crumpled dying man, lonely and frightened and bewildered.

Morelli is then running beside me. We are breathing hard as we race through a storm of machine gun fire to reach that abandoned farmhouse at the intersection north of Steyr, our hearts pumping wildly, surprised that those steel-jacketed metal messengers of death hadn't ripped bloody, ragged paths through our tired, exhausted bodies.

The Austrian sun still seems terribly bright, forcing me to squint, and I can still taste the gritty, swirling dust our jeeps kicked up from the narrow, winding, dirt roads.

Then I'm back with the ghostly caravan riding through the Pine Forest with the horrible stench of death entering my nostrils as I see shadowy corpses rise from the muck and fall back down again.

Tears spring quickly to my eyes as I see McHugh lying in the middle of the road crying for help and slowly bleeding to death as the machine guns and 88s set up a horrible clatter in my ears. I see Ba-ba-balls standing on the Sherman tank, smiling at me, about to tell me how happy he was to see me again, just before being gunned down by the sniper at the dam at Braunau. Once again Morelli's comforting hand is on my shoulder as I hear him quietly say, "He's dead, Zeb."

I don't pull out those weapons as often anymore and my memories lie restlessly interred beneath the gradually gathering years.

Notes

"Reconnaissance" and "The Sound of Drums" won the Lock-wood Literary Prize at Dartmouth College in 1948, both acclaimed by Robert Frost, Poet-in-Residence at that time.

"Reconnaissance" was later published in the *Dartmouth Literary Quarterly* in 1949.

"The Road to Glory?" was first published in *Army Magazine* under the title "Through the Enemy's Lines: A Platoon's Story" in 1989. It was later selected for the anthology "Front & Center" published in 1991, a compilation of the best articles that appeared in *Army Magazine* over the past 50 years.

Bibliography

Ambrose, Stephen E.
1992   *Band of Brothers*. Simon & Schuster.

Cury, Ed C.
1988   *Time Out For War*. Rainbow Books.

D'Este, Carlo
1991   *Fatal Decision*. Harper Collins.

Ellis, John
1990   *Brute Force*. Viking Penguin.
1991   *On the Front Lines*. John Wiley & Sons.

Farago, Ladislas
1981   *The Last Days of Patton*. McGraw.

Hass, Albert
1984   *The Doctor and the Damned*. St. Martin's Press.

Kennett, Lee
1987   *GI: The American Soldier in World War II*. Charles Scribner's S

Lifton, Robert Jay
1986   *The Nazi Doctors*. Basic Books.

Lucas, James
1990   *The Third Reich*. Arms and Armour Press.

McMahon, Gerald
1986   *Farthest East: A History of the 71st Infantry Division*. Yadermar

Moseley, Leonard
1969   *On Borrowed Time*. Random House.

Phibbs, Brendan
1987   *The Other Side of Time*. Little Brown & Co.

Ryan, Cornelius
1966   *The Last Battle*. Simon & Schuster.

Segev, Tom
1987   *Soldiers of Evil*. McGraw Hill.

Shirer, William L.
1969   *The Collapse of the Third Republic*. Simon & Schuster.

Personal communications from the following individuals, all former members of Headquarters Company, 5th Infantry Regiment, 71st Division: Dom Morelli, Norman Rabek, Jack Martin, Ruben Densman, Ed Bowers, Luther Joe Oleson, Elmont Michaelson, Alex Mathisen, Francis Anterhaus, Ralph Monsees, and L.J. Richardson.